The Massey Lectures Series

The Massey Lectures are co-sponsored by Massey College, in the University of Toronto, and CBC Radio. The series was created in honour of the Right Honourable Vincent Massey, former governor general of Canada, and was inaugurated in 1961 to enable distinguished authorities to communicate the results of original study on subjects of contemporary interest.

This book comprises the 1999 Massey Lectures, "The Triumph of Narrative," broadcast in November 1999 as part of CBC Radio's *Ideas* series. The producer of the series was Richard Handler; the executive producer was Bernie Lucht.

Robert Fulford

Robert Fulford has been hailed as "the foremost cultural journalist" in Canada. He has been a journalist since he left high school in 1950 to work as a junior sports writer at the *Globe and Mail*. He was editor of *Saturday Night* magazine for nineteen years and he currently writes a weekly column for the *Globe and Mail* on ideas and a monthly column on media in *Toronto Life*.

He has received honorary degrees from five universities and is an honorary fellow of the Ontario College of Art and Design, a fellow of Massey College, and an officer of the Order of Canada.

ALSO BY ROBERT FULFORD

THE TRIUMPH OF NARRATIVE

*Storytelling
in the Age of Mass
Culture*

ROBERT FULFORD

Published in 1999 by
House of Anansi Press Limited
34 Lesmill Road
Toronto, ON M3B 2T6
Tel. (416) 445-3333
Fax (416) 445-5967
www.anansi.ca

Distributed in Canada by
General Distribution Services Inc.
325 Humber College Blvd.
Etobicoke, ON M9W 7C3
Tel. (416) 213-1919
Fax (416) 213-1917
Email Customer.Service@ccmailgw.genpub.com

CBC logo used by permission

03 02 01 00 99   1 2 3 4 5

CANADIAN CATALOGUING IN PUBLICATION DATA

Fulford, Robert, 1932–
The triumph of narrative: storytelling in the age of mass culture

(CBC Massey lectures series)
ISBN 0-88789-645-9

1. Narration (Rhetoric). 2. Storytelling. 3. Literature and society.
4. Journalism – Social aspects. I. Title II. Series.

PN212.F84 1999   809'.923   C99-931352-5

Cover design: Bill Douglas @ The Bang
Typesetting: Brian Panhuyzen

Printed and bound in Canada

*We acknowledge for their financial support of our publishing program the Canada
Council for the Arts, the Ontario Arts Council, and the Government of Canada
through the Book Publishing Industry Development Program (BPIDP).*

For Rachel Fulford and Sarah Fulford,

beloved listeners, wise storytellers

Contents

PREFACE

STORYTELLING IS THE mother of all literary arts, and anyone who reads must occasionally speculate on its enduring power. My own interest in storytelling has been more than occasional: the questions raised in this book have been central concerns of mine for many years, though I didn't realize how central until I began bringing them together for the first time. Now it seems clear that I have been gathering my thoughts on this immense subject for more than half a century.

The chance to investigate the narrative impulse at some length came when I was appointed the 1999 Massey lecturer by the Canadian Broadcasting Corporation. The Massey Lectures were founded in 1961 to honour Vincent Massey, a major patron of the arts as well as the first Canadian-born governor general. Each autumn, a writer, teacher, or public figure gives a series of five one-hour radio talks on a subject that springs naturally from his or her work. In recent years, Massey College, which

Vincent Massey created, has been associated with the lectures, and the House of Anansi Press has published them.

The form is now traditional — five separate but interlocked lectures, each around 7,500 words. Themes tend to be wide-ranging, such as the pathology of family life, the implications of technology, or the prospects for capitalism in the next century. I discussed several approaches with the CBC and Massey College, and in the end we settled on an exploration of storytelling. It seems to me that this crucial element of culture receives less attention than it deserves; just because it is so pervasive, we often fail to consider its sources and its implications.

Of all the ways we communicate with one another, the story has established itself as the most comfortable, the most versatile — and perhaps also the most dangerous. Stories touch all of us, reaching across cultures and generations, accompanying humanity down the centuries. Assembling facts or incidents into tales is the only form of expression and entertainment that most of us enjoy equally at age three and age seventy-three.

The story links us to ancestors we can never know, people who lived ten or twenty thousand years ago. As the study of preliterate cultures demonstrates, storytelling was central to society long before humans learned to write. Millions of anonymous raconteurs invented narrative, and simultaneously began the history of civilization, when they discovered how to turn their observations and knowledge into tales they could pass on to others.

My plan when I set out to write these lectures was to look at narrative from a few unusual angles and perhaps open it to wider discussion. I especially wanted to assert the value of those unruly and unaccredited forms of narrative that arise from conversation, in particular the stories, true or untrue, that we tell about ourselves and people we know. In my view, we can profitably bring to amateur storytelling the same tools of understanding that we routinely apply to literature.

My first chapter locates the foundations of narrative in gossip, that much maligned art form. It relates gossip to sophisticated fiction, and discusses the personal histories that people concoct in the course of establishing their identity. From this beginning at the bottom of the narrative food chain, my second chapter moves to an arena of grand ambition, where Edward Gibbon, H. G. Wells, Arnold Toynbee, and others have tried to chart the course of civilization with their master narratives. My own profession, journalism, stands at the core of the third chapter, which also discusses the endlessly surprising form of literature that we call urban legends. My fourth chapter deals with the "unreliable narrator," as deployed by writers such as Vladimir Nabokov and Ford Madox Ford; this subject nestles beside postmodern academic theory, each of them commenting on the other. Finally, in chapter five, as a way of relating history to the present moment, I trace one long vibrant line of romantic narrative from Sir Walter Scott's *Ivanhoe* to contemporary mass culture, where the burden of narrative comes to rest on that exceptional figure invented by the twentieth century, the star of movies and television. All this, I hope, serves my main intention: to identify the lines of meaning that connect public narratives, grand or humble, with the narratives we all enact, the true stories of our lives.

It's a pleasure to record several significant debts incurred in the writing of this book. Bernie Lucht, executive producer of the *Ideas* series at the CBC, called me with the welcome news that I was to be the 1999 Massey lecturer; he then helped me to select my topic and develop an outline. Richard Handler, also of *Ideas*, was my excellent coach, conscience, and goad through the writing; he also produced the lectures for radio. I'm grateful to Martha Sharpe of House of Anansi Press for her thoughtful suggestions and to Janice Weaver for her meticulous copyediting. Geraldine Sherman, Sarah Fulford, and Rachel Fulford all read early drafts and returned them with valuable criticisms. Robert Lewis's invitation to write an essay for *Maclean's* pushed me towards this subject. Katherine Ashenburg, John Fraser, and Barbara Moon supplied astute comments, and Richard Landon a helpful piece of research. Margaret Fulford, Webmaster extraordinaire, provided technical support. Beverley Slopen, as always, performed the dual role of agent and cheerleader.

Robert Fulford
Toronto, September 1999
robert.fulford@utoronto.ca

GOSSIP, LITERATURE, AND FICTIONS OF THE SELF

NO DOUBT NARRATIVE began its life on earth in the form of gossip, simple stories told by one individual to another. Gossip remains a folk-art version of literature, the back-fence way of compressing events and exploring their meaning. Like the grander forms of storytelling, gossip expresses our concerns and anxieties, it delivers moral judgements, and it contains ironies and ambiguities that we may only partly understand, just like the most serious work of the greatest authors. When we gossip we judge ourselves as well as those we talk about.

Gossip has always fed literary art. The novelist Mary McCarthy argued, in the famous essay "The Fact in Fiction," that even the most serious novels adopt a tone that resembles gossip. In the first paragraph of *War and Peace*, a woman discusses Napoleon precisely in the style of a gossip. The speech ends, "Sit down and talk to me," and we readers know the gossip will go on. McCarthy pointed out that Tolstoy, Flaubert, Proust, and all the other great novelists speak to us much like neighbours relating scandal: "You will hardly believe what happened next," they all say to us, in effect. "Wait and I'll tell you." She suggested that if a book is entirely untouched by "the breath of scandal," then it's probably not a novel.

Herzog by Saul Bellow, one of the major American books of the last half century, has nothing to fear on that point. *Herzog* emerged out of scandal and carries scandal with it wherever it goes. That does not detract from its stature as a novel; in fact, following McCarthy, it heightens the book's value. But in any case, it demonstrates the close dependence of literature on gossip.

We can pick up the story in the published journal of the late Alfred Kazin, the American literary critic. Kazin held an exalted view of literature's place in society, but he took as much interest in gossip as anyone. His journal, published under the typically grand title *A Lifetime Burning in Every Moment*, outlines the history of a single banal event. He shows how one incident became socially mobile and skipped nimbly up the class levels of literature from the peasantry of gossip to the aristocracy of world literature.

One day in 1964, Kazin wrote in his journal a few words about a woman he had known several years before. She was attractive, rather pretentious, and narcissistic in a way that Kazin found annoying and embarrassing. He wrote, "She was so occupied with herself that if anyone referred to a recent historic happening, she would sweetly ask, sucking a finger, 'Let's see, how old was I then?'" She was drawing attention to herself, but perhaps she was also groping for a connection to history; possibly this habit of hers was related to the feeling we acknowledge when we say we remember where we were when President Kennedy was killed or the first astronaut stepped onto the moon. She was claiming a connection to history, however marginal. But it happens that as she spoke of historic events in this way, she was also acting in history, specifically literary history, as Kazin subsequently learned. The woman in his journal was Alexandra Tschacbasov, also called Sasha, Sandra, or Sondra. In the 1950s, when Kazin knew her, she was the second wife of Saul Bellow. She was also the secret lover of Jack Ludwig, a writer and teacher from Winnipeg.

Ludwig was Bellow's close friend and passionate admirer. The love affair destroyed their friendship and for decades affected the lives of the two lovers, their spouses, their many children and grandchildren, and their friends and acquaintances. It has even touched me distantly, since I'm acquainted with three of the four principals, all but Sasha herself.

It began as a scandal to some, a melancholy incident from married life to others, and a classic bawdy tale to those who saw it from a comfortable distance. But as it moved through the years, this little anecdote added bits of meaning and slowly expanded. In the end, it fulfilled Aristotle's description of narrative: he explained that narrative demands *recognition*, something familiar to us, and also *reversal*, a turn of fortune. In this case, we have adultery and betrayal, and there is nothing more familiar in literature or gossip. And the reversal lies in the fact that the apparently marginal young woman who seemed silly to Kazin was actually at the centre of a story people would be talking about for many years to come.

It touched me mainly as a *story* rather than an experience. There's a difference. A story has shape, outlines, limits; an experience blurs at the edges and tends to merge imperceptibly with related experiences. In many cases, experiences are what happen to us, whereas stories happen to other people. Experiences are intensely complicated and hard to recount: for instance, I could describe the failed first marriages of a dozen friends with far more clarity than I could describe my own. That's because I know too much about my personal history, and lack the distance necessary for simplicity. Stories, in order to *become* stories, must be simplified, stripped of extraneous detail and vagrant feeling. We find it easier to do this with the lives of others — though from time to time, we may apply the same technique to our own history.

Sasha's story interests me partly because of my fascination with the *roman à clef*, the novel with a key, in which "real" people appear in fictional form. When we read about post-war Paris intellectuals in Simone de Beauvoir's *Mandarins*, we understand that the character named Henri Perron stands in certain crucial ways for Albert Camus, and that Robert Dubreuilh represents a version of Jean-Paul Sartre. We also know that the struggle between these two characters is a fictional replay of the real struggle between Camus and Sartre. And when we read D. H. Lawrence's *Women in Love*, we understand that the obnoxious character named Hermione is based on Lawrence's friend Lady Ottoline Morrell, who was mortified when she read the book. Reading a novel that has become known for this quality, we learn to absorb at least two layers of storytelling simultaneously: first, the one created explicitly by the author; second, the story-within-the-story, the *roman à clef*, with all that it implies about interpersonal relations and literary politics. This is gossip transformed into literature.

When Saul Bellow discovered what had happened between his wife and his friend, a *roman à clef* was born. Humiliated, he reacted with a fury so powerful that it provided (as his biographer, James Atlas, has said) the emotional fuel for *Herzog*. He poured his own outrage into the soul of Moses Herzog, an eccentric scholar and cuckolded husband who suffers a nervous crisis. Bellow mercilessly satirizes both his ex-wife and his ex-friend, and as he does so his anger against them moves out in great waves, turning his novel into a tour of American society, a critique of the superficiality of modern life, and a meditation on a favourite Bellow theme — what Herzog calls "this great bone-breaking burden of selfhood and self-development," the load placed on individuals in an age of unbelief.

Herzog touched many readers. When it appeared in September 1964, the *New York Times* reviewer called it a masterpiece. It went on the *Times* best-seller list and stayed there for a year, an astonishing performance for a novel *by* an intellectual *about* an intellectual. As one of the most widely praised books of that period, it helped install Bellow in the pantheon vacated a few years earlier with the deaths of William Faulkner and Ernest Hemingway. Bellow himself described *Herzog* as an expression of the human need to justify one's actions. "Complaining," he said, "is one of the great secular arts. . . . There is a profound human need to be right." A complaint transformed into powerful fiction, *Herzog* helped Bellow win the Nobel Prize for literature in 1976. So the story of Sasha, Saul, and Jack blossomed in ways its original protagonists could never have anticipated. Sasha's connection with *Herzog* has been discussed in print several times, and no doubt will be discussed many times more. Her attention-seeking question about where she was during some historic moment eventually acquired a new answer: she was there; she was *making* literary history, in her way.

Each of us will think of Sasha's story differently, depending perhaps on our views about adultery, love, or how literature should be made. In one way or another, we will see these events in the light of our own principles — because stories inevitably demand ethical understanding. There is no such thing as *just a story*. A story is always charged with meaning, otherwise it is not a story, merely a sequence of events. It may be possible, as social scientists imagine, to create value-free sociology, but there is no such thing as a value-free story. And we can be sure that if we know a story well enough to tell it, then it carries meaning for us. We can say about stories what W. H. Auden said about books — some stories may be unjustly forgotten, but no stories are unjustly remembered. They do not survive through the vagaries of whim. If a story has been swimming in the vast ocean of human consciousness for decades or centuries or even millennia, it has earned its place.

This goes some distance towards explaining what I call the triumph of narrative. In our time, narrative has come under severe attack. The "master narratives" by which our society traditionally guided itself, from the Bible to the agreed-upon stories of beneficial British imperialism and European ascendancy, have been challenged and largely discredited. The Cold War, a narrative that organized the way many people saw the world for more than four decades, has dissolved. Popular narrative on television has come to be seen as the opiate of the masses, the way religion was described long ago. Serious fiction writers are nervous about introducing too-obvious narratives into their books. And yet humanity clings to narrative. We may mistrust large-scale narratives that attempt to shape society, but our narrative drive persists. For all the reasons that fill this book, we cannot do without it.

Stories survive partly because they remind us of what we know and partly because they call us back to what we consider significant. *Hansel and Gretel* reminds us how helpless we felt as children. *Anne of Green Gables* reminds us of the power of imagination in a world that tries to deny its value. *Huckleberry Finn* reminds us of the individual's duty to defy the rules of an unjust world. Orwell's *1984* reminds us of our century's darkest moments, when the individual spirit itself became a crime; conversely, it helps us to remember why we think individualism is central to our way of life.

Stories, however valuable, may be puzzling as well as engaging. Often, even the greatest story may fail at the task it sets for itself — and this applies as much to movies and plays and novels as it does to folk tales handed down from our ancestors. Stories ostensibly begin in order to explain something, or to make an event clear. They turn an incident this way and that, throw several kinds of light on it, surround it with a certain mood — and then put it back in its place, still unexplained. The father of the modern short story, Anton Chekhov, wrote "The Lady with the Dog" a century ago, in 1899. It has since been translated and published again and again all over the world, but no one would claim that it solves the problem it presents — a cold and promiscuous man finds himself falling in love for the first time when it is both inconvenient and too late. At the end, we have no idea what the characters will do or even what they should do. In a few pages, Chekhov leads us to the core of a complex and excruciating dilemma and leaves us there.

Among those who produce films and TV shows, and try to shape novels for the mass market, there's a tendency to make every story explain itself clearly and conclude neatly. It has become a kind of rule that neatness counts in narrative: don't leave the audience wondering. Sometimes we express resentment when this rule is broken. But if that rule actually applied, the Book of Job, to take one spectacular case, would have disappeared from our consciousness long ago. Certainly it makes no ordinary sense. The Book of Job concerns a prosperous man whose faith in God is tested by terrible acts committed against him with the agreement of God. It describes draconian punishments whose rationale we cannot begin to understand, permitted by a god we cannot admire, recounted to us by an author whose identity we cannot know. Yet it remains with us, more than 2,000 years after it was first set down; there's something that makes Job's hideous story, with his boils and his murdered children, more appealing than almost any equivalent in the Western tradition. It lives in daily conversation as much as in the Bible and in literature; people know Job who can't remember anything much about Joshua or Saul. What accounts for its power?

It deals with the most painful human situation — arbitrary suffering — yet to those who are afflicted it offers neither consolation nor understanding. Perhaps that's the very reason it maintains its large place in our collective imagination: implicitly, it tells us that the ways of God, or nature, or whatever force governs life, are unknowable — and it is presumptuous of us to try to know them. Perhaps we return to the Book of Job to remind ourselves that whatever we do, our fate may well be determined by incomprehensible forces.

A story that matters to us, whether it's an ancient story like Job's or a modern story like Herzog's, becomes a bundle in which we wrap truth, hope, and dread. Stories are how we explain, how we teach, how we entertain ourselves, and how we often do all three at once. They are the juncture where facts and feelings meet. And for those reasons, they are central to civilization — in fact, civilization takes form in our minds as a series of narratives.

My own beginnings as a professional in the world of narrative were, to say the least, primitive. As a young reporter, I learned to write news in the awkward, upside-down manner prescribed by the ancient rules of newspapers: you must put all the vital information in the first paragraph, then add decreasingly important facts as you work through your article, until finally you end with a pathetic whimper of inconsequence, the least interesting data being inserted at the bottom for the tiny minority of readers who are still with you.

We reporters always called our newspaper pieces "stories." "Have you finished your story?" "How long will your story run?" But in truth, they were more like inter-office memos than real stories, since they lacked a story's main qualities: suspense, organization, voice, mood, point of view. That newspaper formula, called the inverted pyramid, appeared in the nineteenth century, when telegraphy was erratic and the transmission of an article might be broken off anywhere in the middle; in the first seventy-five years of the twentieth century, it proved convenient for editors who had to cut an article in the composing room and liked to snip off a few paragraphs of type from the bottom, confident they were missing nothing of value. It offers a hasty reader a way to absorb a few facts quickly, but otherwise it's an impossible form of narrative. Telegraphy and lead type, and most other reasons for writing the inverted-pyramid article, have long since vanished, but in many newspapers it remains with us yet, a fragment of nineteenth-century culture that lived through the twentieth century and will certainly survive into the twenty-first.

No sooner had I learned this format than I began thinking of ways to get around it. My hope was eventually to write magazine articles and books, but I was also beginning to realize that when I hear a good story, I have an almost physical need to tell it. In a simple-minded twenty-year-old's way, I began thinking of how I could express that urge in my work. I wanted to write long articles that used some of the techniques of literature, and I began studying journalists who had mastered that trick. After a while, I came to recognize the natural or compulsive storytellers among journalists, and I read every word of theirs I could find. Rebecca West in England, Hector Charlesworth in Canada, and A. J. Liebling in the United States were typical of those to whom I eventually learned to pay careful attention. As I began to write reviews, I studied those critics, such as Bernard Shaw and Edmund Wilson, who used narrative as a way to discuss complicated issues of art and society. And after a time, I learned to light a candle to Lytton Strachey, whose 1918 collection of articles, *Eminent Victorians*, became a kind of textbook on magazine writing. It's often said that he revolutionized the writing of biography, replacing the wordy, dull, and reverential style of the nineteenth century with his swift, sharply critical, and often funny accounts of Victorian lives. He also showed many of us how to write magazine articles by focusing on a shrewd and sometimes daring analysis of the narrative material. Strachey's goal in *Eminent Victorians* was clear: to sweep away the hypocrisy surrounding the lives of certain key figures of the Victorian era, such as Florence Nightingale, the founder of modern nursing, and Thomas Arnold, who more than anyone else was responsible for the development of the elite private schools of England. Strachey's method was to immerse himself in the details of their lives, fix on his theme, and then produce brisk, frank articles assessing their lives. Sometimes, as with Thomas Arnold, Strachey's narrative led us to the conviction that his subject was a failure. Arnold was an "earnest enthusiast who strove to make his pupils Christian gentlemen," but he created a system that leaned heavily on competitive and compulsory games, respectability, and a dictatorship exercised within the school by the more powerful boys. Few young magazine writers today read Strachey, but most of the writers from whom they learned their craft were Strachey readers a generation or two in the past.

Becoming more conscious of my attraction to stories and storytelling, I dimly recognized an impulse that was not entirely rational. I don't mean to suggest a pathology or an obsession; but I came after a while to understand that there was a subconscious stream in my life through which storytelling flowed and affected me, and that I was not always in control of the course this stream took. Malcolm Muggeridge, the British journalist, told a story about himself that illustrates the point. As a British spy in the Second World War, he was travelling through Lisbon, a neutral capital where the British and the Germans maintained embassies and spy networks. Muggeridge was a loyal Englishman, and no admirer of the Nazis, but in Lisbon one day he had a powerful impulse to go to the

German embassy, turn himself in, and tell everything he knew about the British espionage service. Of course, he didn't do it, but when I read this little confession I understood that Muggeridge was writing about me (and perhaps many others) as much as he was writing about himself. I quickened to that idea. I understood the wild perversity of his feeling. He was a storyteller. He wanted to tell stories. And he knew that if he went over to the Germans, it would create an endlessly complicated story. For one moment of insanity, his storytelling drive seemed stronger than all other feelings.

Most of these narratives are public; for instance, Muggeridge recounted that story about his espionage days in his published memoirs. Private stories, our own essential stories, the stories we tell ourselves and others to structure our personal histories and explain who we are, are another matter. These stories, when they take a wrong turn, can leave us terrifyingly alone and expose us to humiliation or worse. They are central to our identity, and if they fail us we may fall apart. Paul Auster, the American novelist, puts it succinctly: "We construct a narrative for ourselves," he says, "and that's the thread we follow from one day to the next. People who disintegrate as personalities are the ones who lose that thread." As Auster sees it, each more or less healthy man or woman has a story that helps create and sustain the necessary integrity of the personality. In some of Auster's novels, such as *City of Glass*, a central character collapses because he loses the thread of his story. Erik Erikson, the psychoanalyst, saw the private story as a necessity in the development of personality. In *Young Man Luther*, Erikson wrote: "To be adult means among other things to see one's own life in continuous perspective, both in retrospect and in prospect."

Most of us feel the need to describe how we came to be what we are. We want to make our stories known, and we want to believe those stories carry value. To discover we have no story is to acknowledge that our existence is meaningless, which we may find unbearable. Charlotte Linde of Stanford University, in her book *Life Stories: The Creation of Coherence*, says: "Life stories express our sense of self — who we are . . . and how we became that person." She thinks they also "communicate our sense of self to others and negotiate it with others."

We might add another level of meaning to what Linde says: when we make stories, when we turn raw events into personal sagas, parables, tales, and anecdotes, we are often struggling to come to terms with one of the inescapably difficult and puzzling facts of existence. Storytelling is an attempt to deal with and at least partly *contain* the terrifyingly haphazard quality of life. Large parts of life, sometimes the most crucial parts, depend on random happenings, contingency. A woman turns a corner, meets a strange man, two years later they marry, they have children together — and in twenty years, there are adults walking the earth who would not have existed if that woman had not turned that corner on that day. The human results of that apparently random event may go on for hundreds or even thousands of years, a single stray moment casting its shadow into an unimaginably long future. We can gaze on this fact with wonder; but we may also grow uneasy in contemplating it, because it emphasizes how little we control the course of our lives.

We can choose to search for a divine intention in everything; or, if we have attained a degree of serenity by some other means, we can simply accept contingency as a beautiful mystery that will always be part of life. Or we may decline to accept it, and instead look for patterns, plots, meanings. That's what stories provide. An anecdote about how grandmother met grandfather may evolve over the years into a piece of narrative, a passage in our family saga. Along the way, it acquires point and meaning because we cannot bear to think that there is no meaningful structure in the way we develop.

The anthropologist Clifford Geertz says that humans are "symbolizing, conceptualizing, meaning-seeking" animals. In our species, he says, "The drive to make sense out of experience, to give it form and order, is evidently as real and as pressing as the more familiar biological needs." To Geertz, a human being is an organism "which cannot live in a world it is unable to understand." But if it is understanding we yearn for, why isn't analysis good enough? Why can't we simply *study* our experience rather than recounting it chronologically?

The answer is that narrative, as opposed to analysis, has the power to mimic the unfolding of reality. Narrative is selective, and may be untrue, but it can produce the feeling of events occurring in time; it seems to be rooted in reality. This is also the reason for the triumph of narrative, its penetration and in some ways its dominance of our collective imagination: with a combination of ancient devices and up-to-the-minute technology, it can appear to replicate life.

Geertz, as an anthropologist, explains how narrative works in a preliterate society. But our civilization experiences something quite different, the effect of mass storytelling on the mass of people. A billion people, it is said, see the TV program "Baywatch." Commercially manufactured narrative has made fantasy a large part of nearly everyone's life. It has placed narrative in a new context, and perhaps put a new kind of pressure on the lives of individuals. Can our own stories compete with the stories we receive through the mass media? All great or notorious people have stories, sometimes worked out for them or imposed upon them by journalists, sometimes created at their bidding by clever ghost writers. Success creates narratives, but so does failure. If a celebrity becomes addicted to narcotics or alcohol, the addiction and its treatment can become a story, rich in pathos and courage. If J. D. Salinger chooses to stop writing for publication and cut himself off from much of humanity, those acts of negation become stories in themselves. Most celebrity stories are built to a traditional design, so that they imply a moral.

How does this affect those who feel they do not possess stories? Is it possible that being continuously surrounded by compelling stories makes us uncomfortable with our own less impressive tales of success and failure? We know that stories create life, even as life throws up stories: in Philip Roth's devious and inventive novel *The Counterlife*, his narrator speaks about "the kind of stories that people turn life into, the kind of lives that people turn stories into." That theme provides Roth with much of his best material: as we read him we understand that we are reading stories about storytelling. One of his major characters, Nathan Zuckerman, a writer much like Roth, tells many of the stories, and sometimes admits that he, a purely fictional character, is further fictionalizing the events he's describing — so that we have fiction within fiction. In this, Zuckerman and Roth seem to be saying that they are much like the rest of humanity, organizing the past so that it makes acceptable sense — perhaps we might go further and say *bearable, endurable* sense.

We can see this going on all around us, or hear it. I once knew a man who described his earlier marriages as movies. "That was in my first movie," he would say. It was a joke, he smiled when he said it, but it was a rueful joke, and I understood that he was trying to package his life story into segments that he could believe were as harmless and manageable as movies.

When the truth about us feels inadequate, we may try to rewrite it, so that it comes closer to what we believe is expected of us. Sometimes people improvise on the facts of their lives, like a jazz musician improvising on a composer's melody. Someone who reinvents a personal past, adding the Oxford degree that always seemed like such a good idea, or even a year spent as a missionary among the lepers, is what the English used to call a romancer, one who deals in extravagant fictions. "Romancer" is a more generous word than "liar"; it acknowledges that there is always art and ingenuity involved in this kind of fantasy, and not necessarily malice or greed.

In the early 1950s, an account of Canadian heroism in wartime Europe came to the attention of the *Reader's Digest* in New York. It was the story of a Calgary businessman, George DuPre, who had spied for British intelligence in occupied France, been captured while working with the Resistance, and endured torture at the hands of the Gestapo without revealing secrets. DuPre had miraculously escaped and was now frequently giving public speeches about his experience, particularly to youth groups. He had a religious message for the young — "You can't have guts without God," he told them. He claimed that it was his faith that gave him the strength to withstand the Gestapo.

His story fired the imagination of the editors at the *Reader's Digest*. They assigned it to Quentin Reynolds, a famous American reporter who had been a prolific correspondent during the Second World War. Reynolds was a man of genial and careless gullibility, the classic case of a journalist who loved a story at least as much as he loved the truth. There's an ancient rule passed down through generations of cynical journalists: "Never let the facts get in the way of a good story." That might have been invented for Quentin Reynolds. Exaggerations and untruths routinely find their way into the public domain through the typewriters, and now the laptops, of reporters like Reynolds.

DuPre went to New York and moved into Reynolds's house for six days of interviewing. Reynolds was deeply impressed, and later went to Calgary to meet people who knew DuPre. He liked and admired his subject, and later emphasized that DuPre never received or demanded money for his experiences. Reynolds thought the story so good that he turned it into a book, and in 1953 Random House published it as *The Man Who Wouldn't Talk*. Shortly after, a veteran of the Royal Canadian Air Force walked into the offices of the *Calgary Herald* and told the editors that he had spent the war with DuPre. He said DuPre had never left Britain and never served with intelligence. This proved to be the case. When confronted, DuPre confessed that he had made it up, all of it, with the help of material he had read in newspapers and magazines. Apparently it had grown in the telling, over six years. As he said, "It snowballed into something so big that I no longer controlled it. It now controlled me."

Bennett Cerf, the publisher, called a press conference to reveal this imposture. He made it into a joke by asking that booksellers transfer *The Man Who Wouldn't Talk* from the non-fiction to the fiction shelves. The newspapers treated the story with sympathy, and in his memoirs Cerf claimed that the book sold better after it was exposed. Later printings carried an introduction in which Reynolds described the deception and a blurb on the cover that described *The Man Who Wouldn't Talk* as a great literary hoax.

So far as I know, DuPre did not leave behind an account of how this happened, but it's not hard to imagine. We can guess that he was a born storyteller, someone who found it easy to organize facts into orderly tales to amuse himself and those around him. And after the Second World War, his world was filled, or so it must have seemed, with people who were able to tell enthralling wartime stories. At that time, the expression "He had a good war" meant that he came home carrying tales of excitement and adventure. Perhaps DuPre couldn't bear to be one of those without stories to tell. He wanted a place in history, and in a sense he found it, though it was in the history of publishing rather than the history of warfare.

There's poignancy in the idea of an individual thwarted by the lack of a good story. We have no term for it: we might call it narrative deprivation, or we might say the person is story-poor. A good story, perhaps, is essential to a sense of self-worth. Not having one will be experienced as a failure that can be dealt with only by creating fictions of the self — and when that happens, we can see the narrative instinct taken to the extreme.

During one week in March 1999, Canadian newspapers happened to discuss two different cases, each instructive and touching in its own way. In the more famous story, the manager of the Toronto Blue Jays, Tim Johnson, was fired for rewriting his personal history. Apparently he began this process nearly three decades ago, around the time of the Vietnam War. His story resembles DuPre's in that it involves wartime experience and lies, but the two stories differ in function. DuPre's fictionalizing was an attempt to give himself distinction and eminence. Johnson's fictionalizing was the work of a man who was rising towards eminence on his talent but felt he needed a better story to sustain his personality.

During the Vietnam War, Johnson spent several winters in the Marine Corps reserve while playing baseball in the summer. He became a sergeant and trained other men to fight, but avoided active service through a deferment arranged by his baseball club. Out of a sense of guilt (as he has explained it), he began inventing stories about serving in Vietnam. He kept it up for years, and after he became the manager of the Toronto Blue Jays in 1998 he used these stories of danger and death to help motivate his players. Perhaps he had come to believe that his true story was not impressive enough to make him a leader of men. So he had radically amended it — and in the end had been caught, with humiliating and professionally disastrous results.

When he was exposed by the *Toronto Star*, he said, "It's a dark shadow I've lived with for twenty-eight years." And Vietnam was not his only fiction — for some reason, he also inserted in his biography false claims that he was an all-American high-school basketball player and had been offered a University of California athletic scholarship. All this came out in the fall of 1998, and the following spring the Blue Jays let him go.

The other case in the newspapers in March concerned the fictionalized life of a civil servant in the Ontario government named Shirley Horkey. As Christie Blatchford told her story in a remarkable piece for the *National Post*, this middle-aged office worker credibly presented herself to her colleagues as a wife and mother. She often spoke of her husband; she displayed photographs of three grown daughters on her desk; and she told little stories about her

family's life, the big house they lived in, and their summer cottage. All of it was fiction. She had never married,
and she lived alone in a townhouse; the young women in
the photographs were nieces. She had rewritten her life in
a more satisfactory format, and at work she delivered
daily reports on this imaginative construction, like a
Victorian novelist writing a book by instalments. Her
story was a peculiar kind of folk art, sustained up to the
last day of her life. She died in a fire at the age of fifty-two,
and her co-workers never knew her true circumstances
until they met her relatives after her death. Then they
learned that they had for years been playing small secondary roles in the elaborate work of fiction that their
friend was living.

The stories of DuPre, the Canadian serviceman, Johnson, the American baseball manager, and Shirley Horkey,
the civil servant, all sound, at least from a distance, like
distorted attempts to come to terms with uncomfortable
lives, to make reality bearable by wrapping it in a blanket
of agreeable invention.

But sometimes the motives of those who fictionalize
the details of their lives are harder to grasp. What if an
individual is living a rich and attractive life yet reworks it
to make it sound still richer and more attractive? In modern intellectual history, Harold Laski stands as the
spectacular case. He was an author and theorist, a professor of political science at the London School of Economics
for a quarter of a century, the chairman of the Labour
Party of Britain in the 1940s, and one of the principal cre-
ators of democratic socialism. He was also a romancer, on

a grand and even baroque scale. Edmund Wilson, the American literary critic, wrote about him in an essay on the letters that Laski exchanged with Oliver Wendell Holmes, the great American judge. As Wilson wrote,

> The great scandal about Harold Laski, regretted by all his friends and sometimes used against him by his enemies, was his habit of unscrupulous romancing. He would freely invent stories that had often no basis whatever in fact about people he did not know but whom he claimed to have met and talked with, exploits that he had not performed, scenes that had never occurred and books that he had never read.

As Wilson pointed out, Laski knew many eminent and famous people and was widely read. But in his letters, he would claim to have met even more eminent people and claim to have read even more books than was the case. Typically, in writing to Holmes, he describes a trip to Germany during which he met a prominent scholar who had, as it happens, died three years earlier. He would describe a tennis game with someone who actually was in another country at the time — and would say he won it. At one point he would say he had read all of Thomas Hardy, and then years later he would mention that he was reading certain of Hardy's books for the first time. Apparently this tendency never got into his published work or his teaching.

What explains it? Edmund Wilson says: "There was always something not quite sound in his relation to practical realities. . . . In some sense, Laski lived in a dream — a dream of actual data, sustained by a real grasp of history, . . . but a dream that did not, nevertheless, quite make the right contact with life."

Perhaps Laski's type is not so uncommon. We all tend to negotiate with what we perceive to be reality. We agree to accept it and acknowledge some part (but never all) of it. If we accept too much, and speak of it too much, perhaps our discomfort will rise to the point where we cannot live with ourselves, and others will find our candour hard to tolerate. If we accept too little, we can shift towards fantasies that will cripple us — or at least embarrass us. Harold Laski's fantasies can be seen as a breakdown in this intricate process of negotiation; possibly he is not a rare exception but one individual among many, one whose romancing became known because his life was so amply documented.

Examples of reinvention that we hear about usually involve the famous or the dead: Laski was dead before the stories I've told were related in public, and during the life of the Toronto civil servant only a few people guessed her secret. But there is a particular fiction of the self that's routinely detected during the storyteller's lifetime. Since the 1970s, medical journals have been publishing articles about Munchausen's Syndrome, a psychological condition that causes a patient to fake illness and repeatedly seek medical treatment, apparently for no reason except the need to be the centre of attention. The patient, when finally persuaded that the doctors can find nothing wrong, typically moves on to another doctor or another hospital. In a related condition, Munchausen's Syndrome by Proxy, parents induce illnesses in their children, apparently for the same reason. This is narrative used as a perverse instrument of status.

On a less ominous level, there's something that's been noticed in recent times by many people who hire professionals — an epidemic of fabricated credentials and life histories. The phenomenon of alien-abduction stories may also owe a great deal to this need to make of one's life a story alive with meaning and excitement. Can it also help explain the bizarre growth of fictionalized stories produced as fact by journalists? At reputable publications, including the *New Republic*, journalists of considerable ability have been discovered inventing incidents and passing them off as reports on reality. Can these be examples of story-fixation running amok?

In any gallery of imaginative and romantic deceptions, Grey Owl deserves a place of importance. His story will be retold as long as the idea of totally committed, twenty-four-hour-a-day fraudulence continues to fascinate us; it has been explored most recently in Richard Attenborough's film, *Grey Owl*, with Pierce Brosnan in the title role. In the 1930s, Grey Owl was the most famous North American Indian alive, a popular author and lecturer, a great advocate of woodland conservation, a subject of intense interest to newspapers and their readers. But of course, he was not an Indian at all.

He grew up as a white Englishman, Archie Belaney, born at Hastings in 1888. A boy who never knew his father, and seems not to have had much to do with his mother, he was raised by two unmarried aunts and did not have a happy time of it. He dreamt of "Red Indians" in far-off Canada; he built a teepee in his backyard; he demonstrated war dances for his friends; he practised creeping silently through the woods; and at the age of eleven, he saw Buffalo Bill Cody's Wild West show on its European tour. When he was eighteen, he went to Canada and slowly turned his fantasies into something closely resembling reality.

He presented himself as the son of an Apache and a Scot; he dyed his hair a convincing black and darkened his skin; he wore leather jackets with fringes and lived among Ojibwa in Canada. He knew intuitively the sort of Native who would appeal to whites, and created his personality accordingly. He grew so famous that he had a private audience at Buckingham Palace with King George VI and the young princesses, Elizabeth and Margaret Rose, and at the end of it he violated all conceivable protocol by clapping the astonished king on the shoulder and saying, "Goodbye, brother, I'll be seeing you." Like every good con man, he knew how to get away with an outrageous gesture.

He seems almost to have convinced himself — or so we might gather from a story that I once heard about him, a story passed on to me by the late John Gray, who was the head of the Macmillan publishing company in Toronto from the 1940s to the 1970s.

In the 1930s, John Gray, as a young Macmillan salesman, was assigned to escort Grey Owl, one of the company's authors, to a dinner in his honour at the King Edward Hotel in Toronto. As they walked towards the elevators, they attracted the attention of some drunks sitting near the door of the beer parlour. One of them looked out and said, "Hey, Chief, where's your squaw?" Grey Owl, furious, wheeled around, his right hand reaching for the knife that he wore at his belt, part of his Ojibwa uniform, along with the fringed buckskin. My friend John stepped in front of Grey Owl and persuaded him to ignore those oafs. But as the two of them continued towards the elevators, Grey Owl said, with absolutely convincing vehemence: "See how it is? In this country I'll never be anything but a *god-damned Indian*." The incident was a tableau of racial conflict, with the drunken bigots playing drunken bigots, the young liberal salesman playing a young liberal salesman, and the Englishman playing the Canadian Native. And only one of them knew that it was a play.

Thirty years later, telling me this story, John Gray shook his head in amusement and wonder. At the time he didn't doubt Grey Owl's ethnic identity for a second, and even in retrospect he didn't doubt the force of the man's emotion. The story of Grey Owl, despite the fact that it was a lie, remains impressive, and even now there are those who point out that he helped create the conservationist movement of his day. A few people knew the truth about Grey Owl when he was alive, but most of the world had no idea who he was until after he died in 1938. In a sense, he brought off a totally successful self-invention. From Archie Belaney's point of view, the tale of Grey Owl turned out to be a fiction of the self with a happy ending.

MASTER NARRATIVES AND TIIE PATTERNS OF HISTORY

HALF A CENTURY AGO, *Time* magazine was the most influential journal in the world, and what mattered most about *Time* was the face on its cover each week. For sheer authority, there was nothing else in the mass media like *Time*'s cover, and there has been nothing like it since. The people who appeared there were automatically considered extremely important and quite possibly great. When they were intellectuals, such as the poet T. S. Eliot or the architect Ludwig Mies van der Rohe, *Time* lifted them from the swampy margins of highbrow discourse and dropped them into the rushing mainstream of popular culture. It was said that someone who appeared on *Time*'s cover was never the same again. Certainly that was true of Arnold Toynbee, the British scholar who had set out to explain the meaning of human history. Toynbee's face appeared on the March 17, 1947, cover, and immediately he became — at least in the public imagination, and at least for a few years — not only a toweringly important historian, but also an indisputably great man.

There is much to be learned about history and historians from the case of Arnold Toynbee. He wrote the stories of civilizations that rose and fell while simultaneously living the story of a thinker who rose and fell. His life and work say a great deal about what we search for when we write and read history.

Toynbee, by studying past civilizations, seemed to have found an explanation of what humanity had accomplished and what it might do in the future. He proposed to explain nothing less than the meaning of collective human life. That's the intellectual equivalent of magic, a wondrous alchemy that seems to be available to historians who are both learned and brilliant. Toynbee wrote a "master narrative," a work of history that scoops up thousands of facts, fits them into a meaningful pattern, and then draws lessons about human conduct. From the eighteenth century until quite recently, this has been one of the principal functions of narrative: to tell great sweeping stories that will inspire and instruct us all.

Years ago, when I first came upon the term "master narrative," it made me think about my own life and the history of jazz. Jazz was the first art form that touched me, aside from literature, and soon after discovering its existence in early adolescence, I began to learn its story. People who love jazz also love to hear that story, like little children with a favourite fairy tale — how jazz began in New Orleans in the first years of the century, moved north on the Mississippi riverboats until eventually it reached Chicago, and then moved on in triumph to New York; how musicians like Louis Armstrong and Sidney Bechet developed their art in New Orleans; how others in the Midwest, such as Bix Beiderbecke and Benny Goodman, learned it from them and made it popular; and how in the 1940s, Dizzy Gillespie and Charlie Parker developed it into the intense art music we call bebop. That simple narrative provided a way to identify specific forms and styles by fitting them into history and geography. But for many of us, it was more than that. It was also a way of beginning to learn about tradition, innovation, corruption, renewal, and many other themes of history in general. For me, this was an opening to worlds far beyond music; I discovered that by analogy, I could apply these patterns in many other fields.

The story of jazz also taught me something about master narratives themselves: that they are often wrong in significant ways. The master narrative of jazz overgeneralized. It telescoped events in ways that distorted facts, and it left out crucial elements, including whole cities where jazz developed. It undervalued certain musicians because they didn't fit into what quickly became the accepted framework. The history of jazz demonstrated both the uses and the misuses of a master narrative: it explained, to me at least, the need for structured understanding, but at the same time it vividly illustrated the unavoidable drawbacks in that kind of thinking. All this happened to me in adolescence. Since then I have seen others learn in the same way from different master narratives, most of them much more far-reaching — the history of democracy, for instance, or feminism, or art, or Christianity.

A master narrative always speaks with the confidence of unalterable and unassailable truth — and yet paradoxically, it is always in the process of being altered. This is true of the chief narrative of Western civilization, the Bible. It is also true of the most important master narrative that arose in the nineteenth century — the theoretical structure imposed on history by Karl Marx — and of Freudian psychology, which presented itself as a narrative that would eventually answer, or at least address, all questions of personality. A master narrative that we find convincing and persuasive differs from other stories in an important way: it swallows us. It is not a play we can see performed, or a painting we can view, or a city we can visit. A master narrative is a dwelling place. We are intended to live in it.

The central project of Arnold Toynbee's life was exceptionally grand, but in certain ways it resembled the goals of other ambitious writers of history, such as Edward Gibbon, Thomas Babington Macaulay, Francis Parkman, Donald Creighton, H. G. Wells, and Oswald Spengler. They set out to "see it whole," whether "it" was the fading of the Roman Empire, with Gibbon; the English seventeenth century, with Macaulay; the contest between France and England for North America, with Parkman; the creation of the Dominion of Canada, with Creighton; the whole sweep of human progress, with Wells; or the inevitable failure of Western civilization, with Spengler.

The self-chosen role of these writers was to build the large narrative contexts that give meaning to specific events — and thus show readers how our own societies fit into history. Often they attempted more than they could manage, and in reading them today we may smile at their presumption. Yet there's also something touching in these mega-histories, something moving in the attempt to make a narrative so powerful that it can explain the sweep of history and even predict the future. The master historians sorted, weighed, compared, and analyzed: they made history so potent that sometimes its stories became the governing myths of societies or classes.

Alasdair MacIntyre, the moral philosopher, says in his book *After Virtue* that humans create their sense of what matters, and how they should act, by referring consciously or unconsciously to the stories they have learned. MacIntyre says, "I can only answer the question, 'What am I to do?' if I can answer the prior question, 'Of what story or stories do I find myself a part?'" Children grow into adults by learning stories, and so do nations and communities. MacIntyre says, "Deprive children of stories and you leave them unscripted, anxious stutterers in their actions as in their words. . . . There is no way to give us an understanding of any society, including our own, except through the stock of stories which constitute its initial dramatic resources." *Peter Pan*, J. M. Barrie's sentimental fantasy, reads like an illustration of MacIntyre's point. Peter describes himself as a lost boy who has not been told stories; that's why he can't grow up and inhabit stories of his own, as others do. He cannot become an adult because he lacks the narrative equipment. At one point he tells Wendy, "I don't know any stories. None of the lost boys know any stories," and Wendy responds, "How perfectly awful."

It is the fate of all children to be conscripted into a drama they did not write but must perform. The way they learn its shape and nature, as MacIntyre explains, is by hearing and reading stories not only about their own families and societies, but also about good but misguided kings, abandoned children, daughters who foil their fathers to marry the men of their dreams, youngest sons who receive no inheritance and must make their own way in the world, eldest sons who waste their inheritance on riotous living — and all the other themes that run through the literature of childhood. In the same way, societies learn how to play out their life stories by absorbing the history that seems relevant to them.

Each society develops a master narrative to which it frequently refers, particularly in moments of crisis. In our time, several Western countries, including Canada and the United States, have used as a master narrative the only sure source of righteousness and moral certainty available to all of us, the Second World War. Events and individuals associated with that war provide us with precedents and analogies. Because Britain and France ceded much of Czechoslovakia to Hitler at the 1938 Munich conference, the word "Munich" has lived in our language for six decades as shorthand for a self-defeating act of appeasement: it's a single word that contains a story with a moral. When President Bush made war on

Iraq, he compared Saddam Hussein with Hitler —
because Bush understood that Hitler's part in history was
known to just about everyone. For the same reason, President Clinton has compared atrocities in the former
Yugoslavia with the Holocaust perpetrated against the
Jews by the Nazis. These analogies are inexact at best, but
we use them because the story — the master narrative —
of our parents' or our grandparents' generation remains
lodged beneath our feelings about how the relations
between states should be conducted.

In recent decades, the idea of a master narrative has
come under deep suspicion. When we speak of master
narratives developed in the past, we now tend to notice
their faults more often than their virtues. Intellectual life,
it sometimes seems, runs on two ruling impulses, each of
which dictates a set of attitudes. One impulse makes us
organize, categorize, and package all knowledge. The
other encourages us to prove that the organization was
badly done, the categories poorly chosen, and the pack-
aging inept — and unfair. The critics of the master
narrative, now much louder and more numerous than its
friends, argue that this broad, sweeping form of history
leaves out or marginalizes much of humanity, and focuses
on a few central figures to the exclusion of less powerful
elements. An old-fashioned account of the British Empire,
for instance, typically sees it from London and regards
overseas populations as secondary elements, just as Gibbon, in writing about the Roman Empire, considers other
societies important mainly for the way they affect Rome
rather than as valuable in their own right. The historian

who works from a master narrative appears to function, metaphorically, as the agent of an empire, sustaining the empire's self-image as the core of the world.

The critique of master narratives reached a climax in 1992, at the 500th anniversary of what historians have traditionally considered the most important event of the Renaissance. Until perhaps twenty years ago, most people of European descent (and many others) appeared to believe that the historic turning point in question could be described accurately, if incompletely, in three words: "Columbus discovered America." But in the ten or so years leading up to 1992, scholars and others changed the status of that sentence from obvious to dubious. Columbus didn't *discover* the Americas, since there were already many people living on these continents. That verb revealed a Eurocentric and imperialistic habit of mind; the repetition of such an error only added to the grievances of peoples who were in the Americas before his time. So in 1992, everything said and done in relation to Columbus was shadowed by a nervous anxiety about giving offence. That controversy illustrated the fact that we structure history in ways we currently find satisfying and comfortable, even if the events in question occurred five centuries in the past. The master narrative centred on Christopher Columbus collapsed because we no longer found its simple outlines truthful or satisfying — and because they embarrassed us.

Academic historians criticize master narratives on more professional grounds, because those who write them often treat facts as props for their theories and thereby fall into misunderstanding and inaccuracy. For much of this century, university history departments have discouraged master narratives. Beginning in the 1940s, the *Annales* school of history in France rose to prominence on the theory that the details of daily life, rather than great events, deserve the historian's most dedicated attention. Social history soon began to spread through academic departments, and many historians made it a point of pride to turn away from narrative in any form. The subjects covered in history courses moved out from the power centres towards the edges. Historians shifted their attention from the mighty to the weak, so that the typical academic historian of recent decades wrote not about cabinet government or warfare or constitution making but about suicide in the Middle Ages, indentured labourers in the nineteenth century, mental hospitals in early modern France, and the abbess who had a love affair with one of the nuns in Renaissance Italy. A friend of mine who teaches history once said that what her graduate students most want to write about are prostitutes and witches, two subjects on which the documentation in many periods is unfortunately close to non-existent.

Some historians so vehemently turned against narrative that they borrowed the statistical methods of the social sciences in order to analyze great masses of data, such as baptismal records and army admittance forms; they gave their approach the name "cliometrics," a word that marries the name of the goddess of history, Clio, to a term for measurement. Niall Ferguson, a much-discussed

British historian and the author of *The Pity of War*, is no cliometrician, but he argues against the habit of treating history as a story. A story, he says, implies that events had to turn out the way they did. It keeps us from understanding that the final result was not preordained. He thinks we learn much more if we try to understand how people living through historic events experienced them. The future for them was a matter of contingency, accident, surprise — all crucial factors in human affairs, but factors we forget when we assemble events into stories. When Napoleon made war on Russia, many people on both sides believed he would win; but as we tell the story, he seems almost an inevitable loser.

The argument against narrative, and against master narratives, can be deeply convincing. Even so, it appears that education depends on narrative. There is a reason we have traditionally seen the past in this way. By imitating our own life experience, narrative gives us a way to absorb past events on an emotional as well as an intellectual level.

We often hear of studies demonstrating that young people know scandalously little about the history of their country or the world. Those who analyze this problem sometimes cite the downfall of historical storytelling as a major cause of ignorance. J. L. Granatstein, a distinguished Canadian historian, says that "Canada's past has lost its way," and that the intellectual elites have abandoned the national history of the country in favour of narrow specialties. Granatstein says: "Gender studies, labour studies, women's history, regional and local history — all are taught and all should be taught. But so should national history, what we might define as political, military, diplomatic, governmental, and policy history." He claims that national history has disappeared completely from some universities and is barely limping along in others.

In Canada we often imagine that this is peculiarly our problem; in fact, something similar arises in many places. A few years ago, a survey found that a third of British children could not identify Winston Churchill. A recent questionnaire given to 22,000 American children showed that six in ten could not come up with even a sketchy idea of how the United States was founded. In response, Lewis Lapham, the editor of *Harper's* magazine, wrote: "The schools have lost the thread of the American narrative." Without that narrative, he argued, the United States can't permanently sustain democratic government. Lapham thinks Americans need their history more than most people, because the United States is founded not on race but on a series of propositions that can be understood only in historical context. Lapham says, "History is only intelligible as narrative, but narrative these days is against the university rules." He thinks that's because narrative is dangerous. If you tell a story, it's hard to avoid making judgements, and judgements can create difficulties — a point we can confirm by studying Gibbon, Macaulay, Parkman, or Creighton, four narrative historians whose works are charged with controversial opinion. Lapham claims that given the bias against the telling of stories, it's astonishing that anybody learns anything at all. Of course, he overstates the point because he's deeply affronted that anyone could question something in which he totally believes: the value of storytelling.

Arnold Toynbee would never have called himself a storyteller, but stories played a large part in the fulfillment of his life's ambitions. As a young man, he yearned for a place among the great historians. When he was studying at Oxford in 1911, he wrote to a friend: "As for Ambition, with a great screaming A, I have got it pretty strong. I want to be a great gigantic historian." About eight years later, he began to see how he could become such a person. Contemplating the monstrous tragedy of the First World War, he thought he noticed something important. As he put it, "The great civilisations . . . may all reveal the same plot, if we analyse them rightly." "Plot" is the key word here, a form of narrative structure. What if you studied all important civilizations, looking for parallels in their development? Would you discover that all of history has an intelligible pattern? The plotline of civilization became Toynbee's great quest. He called his main work *A Study of History* and brought it out in twelve thick volumes, the first in 1934, the last in 1961. He depicted growth, development, and decay in twenty-one distinct civilizations; he argued that a society's health depends on its ability to respond successfully to challenges; he suggested that we need some form of world government; and he claimed that creating a religion is one of the central tasks of a society. As he wrote about Chinese, Islamic, and Indian societies, they began to seem remarkably alike. Soon people in many parts of the world found themselves analyzing social issues of all kinds in the Toynbeean terms of "challenge and response." He wrote in a private letter that he was building "a myth about the meaning of history and also the meaning of life."

This reflected a notably high self-regard, and Toynbee developed a level of vanity equivalent to his ambitions. In a poem that he did not publish in his lifetime but left behind, he compared himself with Thucydides, Dante, and Jesus Christ. He felt he was *called* to write his books, called to the "job of making sense of history."

In 1947 that cover of *Time* made him a prophet and a seer. It coincided with the publication in New York of a one-volume abridgement of his first six volumes. Whittaker Chambers, the journalist who was later to become famous for naming Alger Hiss as a Soviet spy, wrote the *Time* cover story. He went so far as to suggest that Toynbee was supplanting Karl Marx as the best guide to history and the future. Chambers wrote that most Americans had no idea there was a crisis in history, but Toynbee was the man who could tell them. Toynbee believed that Western civilization had been in crisis since the Reformation. It needed a determined and visionary style of leadership, not unlike the leadership that *Time* magazine and its editor, Henry Luce, were urging on the American people. *Time* presented Toynbee's "vision of history as a call to action — American action, accepting the challenge of defending . . . civilization."

The abridged Toynbee became a best-seller, one of those difficult books that tens of thousands of people suddenly decide they can't do without. It sold 130,000 hardcover copies that year and 85,000 more later. Toynbee bestrode the world of ideas like a colossus. In Japan he became the centre of a sizable cult. Naturally, his success prompted historians to take a close look at him, and usually it wasn't a friendly look. Many decided that in their particular specialties, Toynbee had made mistakes of fact or interpretation. As his biographer later said, "An undertow of criticism and disparagement . . . began to gnaw at his reputation." By the late 1950s, it was commonplace to say he was frequently wrong in detail and probably wrong in general. The man who had set out to explain everything was now said to have explained nothing. His *Study of History* was generally regarded as obsolete even before the last volume came off the press. Today, though some of his books remain in print, there are few who read or quote him.

In 1989, fourteen years after Toynbee's death, the British historian Hugh Trevor-Roper said that Toynbee's theory was now dead as a dodo, "a monument of wasted erudition." Hardly anyone would argue with that. And yet Toynbee left behind a residue of meaning. Master narratives that reach a certain level of popularity have that effect. Toynbee's work helped to decentre the Western imagination. Those who read him and talked about him in the 1940s and 1950s found themselves looking at the world in a less provincial way. He nudged us towards the idea that the West should avoid seeing history mainly from London, Paris, or New York. Perhaps, as it filtered down to the public schools, this comparatively new habit of mind has done as much harm as good. His belief in the comparative study of cultures influenced school curricula, and it is now a common complaint that children are encouraged to understand the world before they have begun to understand the countries in which they live. But for good or ill, the approach of Arnold Toynbee remains part of the air we breathe. His master narrative disturbed the Western world's assumptions.

In the hands of a good historian, a work of history seems inevitable. To the reader who spends a few days with Edward Gibbon or Francis Parkman, it may begin to seem that this story could never have been written another way. And yet every historian knows, and most readers of history eventually learn, that each story is constructed, each emphasis chosen, each major character selected by a historian or a team of historians. And the historians in turn are heavily influenced, sometimes in ways they don't entirely understand, by the intellectual tone of the period in which they are writing and by the imagined needs of the people for whom they are writing.

Norman Cantor titled his book about the great medievalist historians of the twentieth century *Inventing the Middle Ages*, a phrase that neatly summarizes the way we think now about the writing of history as a creative act. This isn't to suggest that facts don't matter. They do, and historians must respect them. There are certain facts that cannot be ignored and must be emphasized. A historian writing on the political history of Britain in the early nineteenth century is not at liberty to decide that the Battle of Waterloo is undeserving of comment. But while certain facts and certain ways of emphasizing facts may be essential, the assembling of those facts involves a vast accumulation of choices. The sum of these choices is what we call narrative history.

Over the centuries, historians and philosophers have put together a certain idea about how Western civilization developed. It began in Mesopotamia and Egypt, the Arabs developed our numbers, the Phoenicians the first phonetic alphabet, the Greeks democracy, the Romans large-scale government, the Hebrews a single god and a system of morals, and the Christians a spirituality based on redemption and grounded in a vast international church. The Roman Empire fell and the Dark Ages descended, until the arrival of the Renaissance, then the Age of Science and the Enlightenment, colonialism, the romantic era, modernity, and perhaps something we now call the postmodern age. In this sketchy account, humanity passes civilization down the centuries like a baton in a relay race.

James J. O'Donnell, a professor of classics at the University of Pennsylvania, argues in his recent book, *Avatars of the Word*, that this master narrative is highly arbitrary — for example, deciding to give Greece as prominent a role as we do is questionable. But nevertheless, this account remains, up to the present, the essential background to all discussions of Western culture, even for those who dispute it. Critics may argue with this or that part of it, or rewrite bits of it: still, the master narrative remains, because we have not concocted a credible substitute. But even as we use it, we should remember that it represents a series of choices made over some centuries by people much like us, people anxious to choose appropriate ancestors.

Master narratives often vanish beneath the waves of opinion, as Toynbee's did, but there remains one magnificent exception, *The History of the Decline and Fall of the Roman Empire*, which Edward Gibbon wrote in six volumes, or 3,000 pages, during the 1770s and 1780s. Today it's still respected and read, and every generation brings out new editions and new interpretations. There's a moral force behind Gibbon's work: as one of his recent biographers has said, Gibbon writes as a rabid partisan, but always for the party of humanity. What seems most striking now is Gibbon's tone. It recalls a much-quoted line about history that appears in the prologue to L. P. Hartley's novel, *The Go-Between*: "The past is a foreign country: they do things differently there." But the particular past that we may think of first is not the past of the Romans; it's the eighteenth century, Gibbon's own period. Gibbon writes with a sure-footed intellectual confidence that has apparently vanished from the earth; certainly no serious writer in our time deploys so much easy poise, so much certainty about his ability to reason towards an authoritative conclusion. Modern commentators famous for their arrogant assertiveness, such as George Steiner and V. S. Naipaul, seem diffident in comparison with Gibbon.

He set out to explain the Roman Empire's history from the Emperor Augustus at the beginning of the first century of the Christian Era to the fall of Constantinople, just as the Renaissance was dawning in 1453. As Gibbon wrote his successive volumes he grew more confident; his opinions became firmer and his style more personal. A historical narrative can sometimes convey a whole way of thought, a whole epoch, and that's what happens here. In Gibbon's narrative about antiquity, we can see modern culture springing to life. The irony, the wit, the ruthless weighing of competing theories, the cool distance — all of this seems engagingly modern, and Gibbon as a presence makes himself felt on every page. In this master narrative the modern self, the free-ranging individualist's mind, still a fairly revolutionary idea, can be seen giving one of its most impressive early performances. Even when we are enthralled by his account of the murder of the Emperor Commodus or the failure of the Greeks to use gunpowder properly against the Turks, the thought of this eighteenth-century gentleman writing for us is seldom far from our minds.

Gibbon had an enemy: the belief that God sometimes reached down from heaven and shaped events. As he said when describing accounts of Constantine's life, "Every event, or appearance, or accident, which seems to deviate from the ordinary course of nature, has been rashly ascribed to the immediate action of the Deity." As a man of the Enlightenment, Gibbon believed he could produce a more persuasive narrative of history. He wanted to annul the idea that God routinely played a role in the history of humans. Gibbon was not the first to write history from a secular perspective, but he was the first who made this intention absolutely clear and lived up to it over a work of great length and quality.

Gibbon was writing about an empire in decline from the centre of an empire that was on an upward course. Parallels were obvious, and quotations from his work were read in Parliament as the successive volumes appeared. But he did not claim that we could answer the questions of the present by studying the past. History was not an instrument of policy to him. He wanted to know because he wanted to know, the best of all reasons. He was a "philosophical historian," as he said, and he grounded his philosophy in the Enlightenment ideal of reason and the search for underlying causes or principles. He struggled towards a larger, more expansive, and much more sophisticated understanding of the causes of events. Like all historians, he hoped to make sense of the past, but he believed that we could do that not by imposing a pattern but by searching through the facts for specific explanations of events; usually he found them in the relationship between individuals and the institutions that controlled their societies.

Astonishingly, he seems never to have doubted that he could handle his ocean of material with accuracy and intelligence. As one recent academic admirer said, "It is all the more remarkable for having been written without university affiliation, research assistants, without access to a public library or to critical editions of major classical texts, and without a word processor."

Before Gibbon's work was thirty years old, it was being rewritten for reasons of Victorian piety. In 1826, the Reverend Thomas Bowdler (whose name entered the English language in the verb *bowdlerize*) brought out a

version of Gibbon from which he had carefully elimi-
nated all criticisms of Christianity and all passages
showing what he considered immoral tendencies. Seventy years later, an eminent classical scholar, J. B. Bury,
published an annotated version of Gibbon, thick with
appendices and footnotes that quarrelled with Gibbon's
facts and tried to amend his judgements. In more recent
times, publishers have simply reissued the original with
few changes. *The Decline and Fall* has now become a work
of literature as much as anything else, a work to be
printed just as the author wrote it.

In the middle of the nineteenth century, another master narrator, Thomas Babington Macaulay, was even more
highly regarded than Gibbon had been. In fact, Macaulay
may have been the most popular historian of all time, so
popular that the sales of his books compared with those
of his contemporary, Charles Dickens. He wrote for the
person he called the plain man, and it was said that if you
travelled to distant corners of Australia in the 1870s, you
could find copies of Macaulay's essays in squatters' huts,
alongside the Bible and Shakespeare. There were clubs all
over England where working men gathered to hear
Macaulay's histories read aloud. His genius lay in his
ability to recreate historic events as powerful narratives,
and to recreate the visual effect of their background; he
combined the qualities of playwright and set designer. I
can pick up a collection of Macaulay's writings, open it
almost anywhere, and find myself drawn into a thrilling
passage on the Battle of the Boyne, or Machiavelli, or
William Pitt the Younger. His greatest work was on the

seventeenth century, *The History of England from the Accession of James the Second*, in five volumes.

Macaulay engaged his mind and spirit with his subject, and communicated that engagement to his readers. He was a man of infinite confidence. Viscount Melbourne is said to have remarked, "I wish I was as cocksure of anything as Tom Macaulay is of everything," which may not have been the first use of that line but was one of the most apt. Beyond his confidence, it was important to Macaulay that he express his moral response to whatever he wrote about.

His reputation eventually collapsed under the weight of that same quality. Because he was so engaged he was also deeply opinionated, and his books seemed altogether credible only to those who shared his opinions. He seemed to imply, in writing of history, that the main purpose of past events had been to create the society of which Macaulay was a member. He was a Protestant and a Whig, and his readers were never allowed to forget it. He believed in progress, reason, and the values of the middle class. In one work he wrote: "The general effect of this . . . narrative will be to excite thankfulness in all religious minds, and hope in the breasts of all patriots. For the history of our country during the last hundred and sixty years is eminently the history of physical, of moral, and of intellectual improvement." He dated the spread of progress from the beginnings of the Protestant Reformation.

His critics often called Macaulay smug, sometimes during his lifetime and more often in later years, when

the Victorian period lost its lustre and liberal optimism —
Whig history — began to seem fatuous. Like other
authors of master narratives, Macaulay portrayed history
with a purpose; once people began questioning that purpose, Macaulay's works lost much of their meaning. In
the end, his example did as much as anything to give the
master narrative a bad name.

Francis Parkman, on the other hand, gives it a good
name, but perhaps despite himself. A Boston aristocrat of
great literary talent, he wrote what he described as "the
history of the American forest," and did it in a way that
was clearly intended to shape the ideas of North Americans about how their societies had developed. He
admired Gibbon's work, and early in his life he began to
glimpse the outlines of a largely unknown saga that took
place on the North American continent in the seventeenth
and eighteenth centuries; he imagined that it might well
justify as much attention as Gibbon gave the Roman
Empire.

Between the 1860s and the early 1890s, Parkman
poured out a series of books with titles such as *Count
Frontenac and New France under Louis XIV, Montcalm and
Wolfe,* and *A Half-Century of Conflict.* His grand overall
subject was the struggle between France and England for
North America in the eighteenth century, a struggle that,
in his view, was won by the right side. Parkman spent
years in the archives, and years walking the trails where
Natives, Frenchmen, and Englishmen struggled for control of the continent. He looked on the silent forests with
a sense of awe that he passed on to his readers. He

reimagined what had happened within these dense sylvan landscapes in the years of conflict. Parkman wrote in a dramatic, rushing style, far more romantic than Gibbon's. This is how he described old-regime France imposing its rules on the colony established on the St. Lawrence:

> Here was a bold attempt to crush under the exactions of a grasping hierarchy, to stifle under the curbs and trappings of a feudal monarchy, a people compassed by influences of the wildest freedom, — whose schools were the forest and the sea, whose trade was an armed barter with savages, and whose daily life a lesson of lawless independence.

Parkman shared none of Gibbon's cool distance, and none of his reticence. Prime Minister Mackenzie King once said, "No country has ever been more fortunate than has Canada in having Parkman to record her history." But Canada has not often expressed its gratitude, and Parkman has never been hugely successful in this country. His views were not entirely fashionable when he set them down, and they have grown steadily less fashionable over the years. Between the French and the English, Parkman came down too quickly and inevitably on the side of the English — no matter how much he admired the French spirit. He also made it plain that he considered Protestants morally superior to Catholics. He accepted too easily a view of the Natives as simple savages — even when his narrative indicated how complex they were. He thought that the Acadians, rather than being purely the victims of English tyranny, to some extent brought their troubles on themselves. Yet Parkman lives as a writer in a way that Macaulay does not. Perhaps because his style is more his own, or perhaps because his subject is less frequently visited than Macaulay's, Parkman feels fresh and invigorating. In recent years, his most important books have been collected and published in two volumes of the Library of America series, a testimony to his literary status, if not to his value as a historian.

The admirers of Donald Creighton hope for a similar revival of his work. Creighton, who died in 1979, was a University of Toronto teacher all his life, and a writer of great distinction for about four decades. In 1937 he staked his first claim to be the national historian of Canada with *The Commercial Empire of the St. Lawrence*. That book, with its account of the fur trade, began the process of turning Canadian history into a powerful narrative. In Creighton's hands, Canada was not an overseas extension of Britain or a northern appendage of the United States but a nation that developed naturally along east-west lines. This became known as the Laurentian Thesis, and it governed much of what was thought and said about Canadian history in the following generations — in the schools, in popular books, and in the mass media. Creighton went on to write his two-volume biography of John A. Macdonald. His work set a pattern for thinking about Canada, which was reflected in the books of Peter C. Newman, Pierre Berton, and many others.

Creighton was an angry nationalist and a passionate anti-American, and he did not hesitate to connect his historical ideas with current affairs. In that sense, he anticipated the nationalist movement that began in English Canada in the late 1960s and retains considerable strength today. But in other ways, Creighton, like Macaulay and Parkman, has suffered through his association with current events. Creighton was a centralist, and in recent times regionalism in several forms has become a potent element in Canadian affairs. Creighton's great virtue was his certainty, his powerful sense that he had an important story to tell and would insist on telling it; but the very passion of his storytelling left him open to attack. Like Toynbee, though on a much smaller scale, he attracted the criticism of professional historians who felt he did not understand their specialties well enough to pronounce on them.

Gibbon, Macaulay, Parkman, Creighton: we could class all of them as professional historians. But sometimes the master narratives come from authors who are not identified with the writing of history. About eighty years ago two attempts at a master narrative appeared, each with a radically different view, yet each in its way a typical twentieth-century response to history. The more optimistic, and the more immediately successful, was *The Outline of History* by H. G. Wells. The more influential was *The Decline of the West* by Oswald Spengler.

H. G. Wells, the celebrated novelist and pioneer science-fiction writer, wrote his book out of scientific optimism and a belief that he could help cure the most serious ills of the world, as Europe had recently revealed them in the First World War. Wells believed in the coming

unity of mankind, but he was convinced that humanity
could never be united so long as it continued to see history in so many different ways. In his mind, *The Outline of
History* was itself a historic event, a milestone on the road
to world government and Utopia. Wells was always
among the most prolific of authors, but on this work he
surpassed himself: he wrote his thousand-page book in
one year. He had a platoon of assistants, whose help he
acknowledged only furtively, and he made free use of the
Encyclopedia Britannica. Even so, it was a prodigious enterprise, with a spectacularly Wellsian argument.

Wells was trying to fill the vacuum opened up by the
displacement of the Bible as the central book of Western
civilization. In Europe, from the time of Martin Luther,
the Bible embodied historical and spiritual truth. It
was the book of books, the narrative of narratives: no stories were as important as the stories it told. But in the
eighteenth and nineteenth centuries, a movement called
the higher criticism began to bring the Bible before the bar
of science. This was the last place the Bible expected to
find itself; it was the Bible that had traditionally judged
science, not the reverse. But the higher criticism grew
steadily stronger and the Bible's authority weaker. For
decades, one of the major scholarly activities of Europe
was taking apart the books of the Bible and reclassifying
them as to their historical accuracy, the validity of the
texts from which they were drawn, and the identity of
their authors.

The higher criticism became a vast international project that left no one untouched. Though it began in many

cases as an act of piety, it effectively moved biblical scholarship beyond the power of the churches; and in the end,
the Bible's ancient power was left in tatters. Our own time
has produced a parallel to the higher criticism in the form
of postmodern theory. In outline, the two movements
sound the same: the frequent statement of ideas that had
been considered unthinkable only recently; the outrage of
those whose most precious beliefs are being assailed; the
learned critics squabbling among themselves; and finally,
the diffusion of the movement's ideas through society
and the slowly dawning recognition that certain propositions are not the fad they once seemed but have woven
themselves into the fabric of intellectual life and even
everyday conversation.

In an atmosphere of loss and renewed intellectual
energy, H. G. Wells set to work. Replacing biblical knowledge with science, he saw humans from the standpoint of
a biologist: as creatures slowly creating themselves,
moving steadily upward towards speech and self-
consciousness, and then further upward towards
advanced stages of human organization. He seized on
every move towards sociability and co-operation as a
sign of the world government that was to come. He lin-
gered over imaginary accounts of agriculture being
invented. He was optimistic like Macaulay, and like
Macaulay he enjoyed setting the scene.

At one point, he placed a drama of ritual human sacri-
fice on the uplands of Wiltshire. He imagined it:

A process through the avenue of stone, of priests, perhaps
fantastically dressed with skins and horns and horrible
painted masks, . . . of chiefs in skins adorned with neck-
laces of teeth and bearing spears and axes, their great
heads of hair held up with pins of bone, of women in skins
or flaxen robes. . . . A certain festival cheerfulness prevails.
And amidst the throng march the appointed human victims, submissive, helpless, staring towards the distant
smoking altar at which they are to die — that the harvests
may be good and the tribe increase. . . . To that had life pro-
gressed 3,000 or 4,000 years ago from its starting-place in
the slime of the tidal beaches.

He believed he was delivering the first general
account of the world's progress. In the empire of Alexan-
der the Great, Wells saw one of many early attempts to
make the international organization that would one day
rule the planet. Humanity had admittedly made many
errors on the way to total world unity, but as Wells wrote,
"The hope of men rises again . . . after every disaster." He
had none of the historian's scruples about leaping to con-
clusions. He could understand everything he learned.
Science, moral righteousness, and a human common-
wealth — those, he decided, were the three ideas that had
lain beneath all human aspiration for thousands of years.
Wells had pulled himself up from a wretched beginning
to a place in the sun of literature and public affairs. Now
he saw humanity, in his own image, following the same
course. He and the species were one.

But a vein of anger also ran through his book; he hated

all those leaders who had come close to creating world government but had failed through their own weakness. He hated Napoleon worst of all. Napoleon could have created a new age for humanity but instead fell prey to his own "self-conceit, . . . vanity, greed and cunning."

Wells imagined himself the champion of what he called the common man, and in his prophecies it was the common man who would triumph. Looking ahead from 1920, Wells saw that nationalism had no future, religion was heading towards total obsolescence, and politics would soon stand revealed as the marginal nuisance it had been for a long time. Soon the whole planet would be called the United States of the World. You could draw from the pages of this one book a long list of the mistaken notions commonly held by the articulate classes eighty years ago.

But *The Outline of History* was hugely successful in many languages and in its day widely respected. E. M. Forster called it a great book, and it was praised as a "magnificent intellectual achievement" by the young Arnold Toynbee, who was just then setting out on his own tour through the past.

Oswald Spengler, like Wells, looked to biology for metaphors, and to individual human lives for analogies. But otherwise he saw everything in a different light. The Wellsian view of humanity ascending towards Utopia was nowhere to be found in Spengler. Human cultures were his historic subject — their rise, their decline, and the stages they go through. His story played itself out again and again, in different places. A culture's history, he reasoned, runs like the "age-phases of the individual man." Cultures realize the potential that is in them; then, in the normal course of things, they die. As much as any single writer, Spengler taught the modern world to think deliberately in analogies and metaphors, and to look for patterns in what seems at times to be an entirely unpatterned universe.

Spengler was a German schoolteacher who brought out in 1918 the first of two volumes that together became *The Decline of the West*. At the beginning of its life, Spengler's thesis was taken by many of his fellow Germans as an explanation of their national misery following their humiliating defeat in the First World War, but his goals were far broader. He understood that most of humanity sees history in a sort of mythological outline; he wanted to change the shape and nature of the myth. To some extent, he did. Like Toynbee, he left something of himself behind, installed in the common mentality of the century. People who have never read *The Decline of the West*, or perhaps even heard the title or the author's name, are affected by it to this moment.

Northrop Frye, the great literary critic, was no admirer of Spengler's right-wing German nationalism, but he nevertheless acknowledged that he had been influenced by Spengler — and so had everyone else. In 1976 Frye wrote: "Everybody thinks in terms of a 'Western' culture to which Europeans and Americans belong; everybody thinks of that culture as old, not young; everybody realizes that its most striking parallels are with the Roman period of Classical culture." And all those thoughts, as Frye said, are Spenglerian. Furthermore, "The decline, or ageing, of the West is as much a part of our mental outlook as the electron or the dinosaur, and in that sense we are all Spenglerians." No one today believes the world is young, as Wells did; just about everyone sees it as old, or at the very least mature. In the contest waged in the 1920s by Wells and Spengler, Spengler emerged the winner.

Perhaps that was because the story he concocted, whether we now think it true or not, was so much more credible — and because it answered one of the questions we continually ask about history: how can we deal with the fact that world-shaking events appear to occur at random? In the seventeenth century, Blaise Pascal summed up this infinitely disturbing aspect of history when he wrote, "Cleopatra's nose: if it had been shorter the whole face of the earth would have been different." Had Cleopatra not been beautiful, and thereby attracted the love of Mark Antony, the history of Rome and Egypt, and therefore the history of civilization, would have developed in another way.

People who have learned to be purposeful in their own lives, and have learned to see causal connections between one event and another, find this truth painful. That pain can be relieved if we see a pattern in history, even if (as with Spengler) it's a cyclical pattern of inevitable rise and decline. Like religion, the idea of inevitability speaks to our anxiety about history, our need to understand why life unfolds as it does. Of course, it can lead us towards pessimism. But if we are searching mainly for a pattern, trying to see sense in otherwise incomprehensible events, we may decide that a pattern that encourages pessimism is better than no pattern at all.

This is not a great time in history for the master narrative, and we may begin to think of it as an artifact of the past, once useful but no longer valuable, like a typewriter. We are tempted to conclude that because the world has learned so much about itself, no similar attempt will be made in the future. Even so, my guess is that we have not heard the end of it. Perhaps those grand histories misled us at times; certainly they demonstrated a breathtaking arrogance. And they have chastened the scholars of today, so that when new books appear with titles such as *History of the World* they seldom claim to find patterns like those of Wells or Toynbee. When J. M. Roberts of Oxford brought out a 983-page book under that title in 1976, he said that in thinking about the future, those who study history have only one advantage: "One may be a little less surprised by the outcome, whatever it is." He asked on the last page whether humanity's experience through history has given us the intellectual ability to survive the threats to our existence. He answered, "There are no grounds for unequivocal assertions one way or another."

But the authors of master narratives, notably Gibbon and Parkman, created works of literature that continue to find many new readers and probably deserve even more. It is also true that these wildly ambitious writers, such as Toynbee and Spengler, have developed conceptual tools that we find useful to this moment. More than that, the thirst we readers demonstrate for universal certainties has lasted so long and expressed itself so often that it seems likely scholars will find new ways to satisfy it.

The need to shape the past as a coherent narrative will not leave us, no matter how many disappointments we endure. The philosopher Arthur Danto has compared the past with "a bin in which are located . . . all the events which have ever happened. It . . . grows moment by moment longer in the forward direction, and moment by moment fuller as layer upon layer of events enter its fluid, accommodating maw." And of course, modern record-keeping being infinitely superior to the record-keeping of the past, the contents of the bin are growing faster than ever before. That alone makes the idea of a master narrative daunting. Nevertheless, it seems likely that at this moment some historian somewhere, ingenious and brave as well as foolish, is digging through the bin of the past with every intention of emerging, manuscript in hand, to issue a blunt, proud declaration to the world — "Here! This is what it all means."

THE LITERATURE OF THE STREETS AND THE SHAPING OF NEWS

SOMEONE ONCE TOLD ME a bizarre little anecdote about revenge. It took place in Oakville, a western suburb of Toronto. The driver of a cement truck, out to make a delivery, stopped by his house unexpectedly in the middle of the day. He found a Cadillac convertible in his driveway, and when he looked in the window he saw his wife and the owner of the car in what used to be called a compromising position. The driver's vengeance was swift. Since his truck was full of ready-mix cement, he emptied it onto the Cadillac. At this point, the man telling me the story paused to describe in loving detail the total destruction of seats, dashboard, and chassis, and finally the wheels collapsing under tons of concrete as the tires popped. The story ended with the truck driver, having utterly destroyed the Cadillac, returning to work.

I think I believed that story; certainly I enjoyed it. But Pierre Berton, who was writing a daily column in the *Toronto Star*, suspected that it was too good to be true and set out to investigate. The person who told him about it said he knew someone who knew the cement-delivery man, so Berton started phoning those people. The connection turned out to be less clear than it seemed at first. The driver was in fact a friend of a friend's friend — and the friend's friend didn't really know the driver either. The leads grew fainter, until finally someone said he couldn't remember where he had heard it. Berton explained in his column that this was of course an urban legend, one of those stories that arise from time to time, their origins almost always obscure.

The urban legend, the most popular living form of folk narrative, persists among us as unconscious literary art, the spontaneous efflorescence of the popular imagination. It reminds us that in certain ways, sophisticated city dwellers remain connected to the ancient roots of narrative; and it demonstrates that we still require stories that we can possess outside the range of the mass media, stories to which we can perhaps make a quiet contribution. In this form of mythology, we also demand the element of intimacy: one thing I've noticed is that the typical urban legend claims to be close to us in space and time. Usually it happened quite recently, it happened nearby, and it happened to someone fairly close to the person telling it. In my experience, no urban legend has ever taken place more than one hundred kilometres from the place where it was told; sometimes it occurred only blocks away.

If we ask who creates these stories, the answer is everyone who tells them. Each of us becomes a fabulator, a myth-maker, since each of us alters the story, at least slightly, perhaps by intention and perhaps by accident. Is there anyone who has not made even a slight improvement when passing along a story? Can anyone claim never to have thrown in an extra detail to heighten verisimilitude, or added a little speculation on the motives of the characters in the stories, speculation that in repeated telling hardened into apparent fact? But how do these stories start, and how do they acquire their often perfect structure? My guess is that each begins as a misunderstanding of something overheard or read. Then the hidden hand takes over, the obscure working of unintentional collective invention. What begins as a fact or two slowly grows into a small work of fiction.

There's something grotesque and at the same time touching about an urban legend: it's as unpredictable as a riot and as anonymous as a prehistoric megalith. It provides a glimpse of the inner lives being lived around us. The glimpse will always be brief and tantalizing, like a landscape revealed for an instant by lightning, but it suggests a wondrous richness, a splendid variety. It rebukes glib assumptions about the blandness of our fellow citizens.

In recent generations the urban legend has replaced the tall tale, which was once a staple of conversational entertainment in various parts of North America. Seventy years ago, Zora Neale Hurston, the novelist and folklorist, made a collection of tall tales by spending eighteen months listening to the old men in her home town of Eatonville, Florida, as they told each other stories. She wrote, "As early as I could remember it was the habit of the men . . . to gather on the . . . porches . . . and swap stories." In the process, some of the men became virtuosos of the fable. Sometimes they frankly called the stories "lyings." In 1935 she brought out a path-breaking volume of black American folklore, *Mules and Men*, a book filled with wonderfully offhand displays of imagination.

Her equivalent on the subject of urban legends is a University of Utah folklorist, Jan Harold Brunvand, a collector of stories and the author of five books in this field. In the early summer of 1961, shortly after he received his doctorate in folklore, Brunvand was told by a neighbour in Michigan about a cement-truck driver from the nearby town of Kalamazoo. This was around the same time I heard the story in Toronto, but the Kalamazoo version differed in one way: the Michigan driver's jealousy was ill-founded, because the Cadillac standing in the driveway was in fact a present his wife had bought him, with her own hard-earned cash; the visitor wasn't a lover, just a car dealer handing over the papers. So in this version, not a common one, the overly suspicious husband destroys his own car.

Brunvand later learned that a paper describing a similar load-of-concrete episode had been read at the Texas Folklore Society a year before he heard it in Michigan. And later in 1961, a roughly identical incident was noted in the *Oregon Folklore Bulletin*. That in turn prompted reports from elsewhere, and by 1962 the Oregon scholars had assembled forty-three separate versions from across the continent. A couple of years later I saw this fable seriously reported in *Private Eye* magazine in England, in a column called "True Stories." Otherwise, it dropped from sight, apparently consigned to the limbo of worn-out myths, like the one about the old woman accidentally microwaving her poodle or the alligators living in the sewers of New York.

But there was still life in the old legend. Ten years passed, and in 1973, in the Norwegian city of Bergen, the *Arbeiderblad* newspaper carried a story headed "Terrible Revenge of a Lover." And here he was again, the driver with the cement truck. He was passing his own home, an apartment building this time, when he noticed a friend's car parked there. He entered his apartment and heard his wife and the friend together in the bedroom. He went outside, drew back the sunroof on the car, and poured into it two cubic metres of cement. (This story usually includes the exact amount of cement used, sometimes in cubic metres, sometimes in tons. In narrative, precise detail can give legitimacy to even the most outlandish tale.)

When that Norwegian newspaper story was picked up by wire services, more details appeared: the friend's car was a 1966 Volkswagen, for instance. The story travelled abroad and appeared in newspapers as far away as Nairobi. Back in Bergen, meanwhile, a rival newspaper carefully established that it was fiction. And finally, the paper that originally ran it admitted being taken in by what it now called an "international journalistic joke." But even as a hoax, it lived on in Bergen. That spring someone with a surrealistic sense of humour filled a real Volkswagen with real cement and pulled it through the streets of the city as a float in the Independence Day parade, legend transformed into literal fact.

All versions have one interesting point in common: no one notices the truck driver as he pours the cement, and the adulterous lover doesn't find out till later about the ruin of his car. This alone would seem to raise a serious problem of credibility. Emptying a cement truck makes so much noise that doing it discreetly in a residential neighbourhood would be impossible.

Then why have so many of us believed it?

We know there is no such thing as "just a story," and this applies as much to urban legends as to any other kind of fable. What is there in this one that's so powerful it drowns out the noise of the cement truck? Perhaps it's the thought of an adulterer being punished. Perhaps our egalitarian spirit quickens to the idea of a blue-collar worker wreaking vengeance on someone who owns a Cadillac. Possibly we delight in the driver's ingenuity. In any case, experience suggests that we tend not to view urban legends with suspicion. As Jan Harold Brunvand says, "The lack of verification in no way diminishes the appeal. . . ." Clearly, the gratification we feel disarms scepticism. It may be that the telling and the listening together amount to a collaborative pleasure that no one wants to mar with harsh discussions of proof or likelihood. Telling the legend gives the narrator a sense of control and the listener a briefly intimate relationship with remarkable events. The will to power expresses itself in this process. The fact of *knowing* is cherished; so is one's ability to display this knowledge.

New urban legends continue to race through society. A recent favourite involves organ-snatching: an out-of-town businessman gets drunk with a prostitute, blacks out, and wakes up with a kidney missing, the delicate and complicated removal operation having been performed while he was deeply anesthetized. Some time ago in South Africa, a legend spread about a pattern of fatalities among patients on life-support. It seems deaths were occurring at the same time every week. Eventually they were traced to a cleaning woman who came into the intensive care unit and unplugged the life-support system so that she could plug in her floor-waxer. This tale travelled from city to city across South Africa, and was always ascribed to a specifically named newspaper, which turned out to have published no such article. This was apparently a case of a metaphor escaping from its cage and running amok: the colloquial phrase for ending an artificially extended life, "pulling the plug," had been transformed into a fable. This story, too, appeared in *Private Eye.*

Half a century ago, I was told that manufacturers had invented a light bulb that would burn forever; they were withholding it because it would destroy their market. Even so, a few prototypes had accidentally escaped from the factories and were being used by certain lucky people, despite the manufacturers' attempts to get them back. Brunvand has frequently collected a similar story, involving a car that runs for a thousand miles on one gallon of gas. Again, a prototype has somehow slipped out of the factory and the makers — fearful that the gasoline industry will be ruined — are desperate to retrieve it.

These tales now float effortlessly through the Internet, but the Internet can't be blamed for them: long before any of us hooked up to the World Wide Web, urban legends rushed like the wind across the continent; today, contributors to the Internet are as likely to debunk fantasies as to promote them.

Many urban legends are harmless, but others inject a kind of poison into the system of human understanding. The legend of the stolen kidneys, for instance, has spread through the Third World and seriously inhibited the growth of international adoption; fictional narratives have encouraged it, notably an episode of "Law & Order" on television and the Brazilian film *Central Station*. If large numbers of people in a given country believe that foreigners are adopting children to steal their organs, governments respond by curtailing or eliminating the international adoption program, to the detriment of children and potential adoptive parents.

The urban legend is a kind of self-generated journalism, a way of wrapping in a narrative package certain observations and anxieties, such as the unspoken terrors of organ transplants or the belief that anonymous corporations conspire to manipulate us. These are narratives in which we can install our feelings of dread; perhaps we use them as a way to sort out and settle our confused responses to events. This literature of the streets, chaotic and unregulated, mirrors in a distorted way the journalism we read, watch on television, and hear on the radio.

The urban legend parodies our desire to have the world explained in the form of stories.

Vast global organizations exist to satisfy this desire with newspapers, magazines, twenty-four-hour news channels, and Internet news sources. The flow of narrative reports is now so much a part of contemporary life that we can hardly imagine doing without it. And yet, pervasive news coverage is less than two centuries old.

The invention of news, and the development of news stories as commodities, constituted one of the momentous turns in the history of the human imagination. It gave humanity a new way to assemble facts, stories, and ideas — a frame, a grid in which to place and assimilate events.

Journalism began with scattered pamphlets, monthlies, and weeklies, often filled with scandal, sometimes scurrilous, but frequently informative. For the early papers in London, what modern publishers call the pass-along readership was phenomenal; roughly twenty individuals read every copy. That was the result of the coffeehouse culture, the "penny university"; you could pay a penny for a cup of coffee and read all the publications the owner of the coffeehouse had acquired.

Those publications led eventually to the creation of the *daily* newspaper, an innovation in news that was probably more significant than any development since. The daily paper embodied a fundamental change in public understanding; its creation represented the crossing of a great divide. The philosopher Hegel, who saw it in an early stage, said that the ritual reading of the newspaper was a secular equivalent of morning prayer. Certainly newspaper reading increased as Bible reading declined. We replaced the stories of the prophets with stories about wondrous events and personalities in the world around us. And just like a religion, newspapers produced enormous changes in the people. New forms of curiosity appeared, new forms of knowledge, and eventually new communities based on shared understanding of politics, business, sports, and more specialized subjects.

Civilization moved slowly into this territory. Daily newspapers didn't quickly become successful and prominent, like video cassettes or the Internet. It took more than a century for the daily to establish itself, and much longer than that to develop into the form we know today. In 1702, a few years after the ending of official press censorship in England, Samuel Buckley established the London *Daily Courant* as a way to make a profit on the flow of information coming from France about the War of the Spanish Succession. His brilliant idea was not quickly imitated. Half a century later, there were only five daily papers in London, each of them just four pages, each of them selling about 1,500 copies — which would mean they had perhaps 30,000 readers each. France acquired its first daily in 1777, the United States in 1784, Canada about fifty years later. These all operated on a small scale. The thick, narrative-filled, advertising-crammed newspaper of today didn't become possible until the rise of mass literacy and the invention of the linotype machine, both of them late in the nineteenth century.

Those early papers created the idea of information as a

continuous flow. Instead of arriving in bits and pieces, as official proclamations or furtive rumours, information now appeared as regularly as the sunrise. Each day, journalists broke off a piece of history, put it on newsprint, and sold it to the public. They created a new habit or addiction, newspaper reading, and established a new mental space. And they didn't do it entirely with pure, high-toned, essential information. Their motives were often crass, their material often vulgar. We publicly fret these days about journalism turning into entertainment, but entertainment has always been a crucial element in journalism: early newspapers were no more staid than the papers of today. Looking recently at the London *Daily Courant* for February 5, 1731, I discovered that the foreign news concentrated on family scandal among the cardinals in Rome and devious political manoeuvring around the emperor in Vienna. There was also a front-page poem, a pioneering piece of media self-criticism titled "The Journalists Displayed." It described the content of newspapers in 1731 as "Bribery! Knavery! Irruptions, Corruptions, and Some-Body's Fall; . . . Removes and Disgraces, and Something and Nothing, and the Devil and all." It went on to say, "When you've read one of 'em, then you've read all" — which suggests that a cynical view of journalism, far from being an invention of our age, is at least 268 years old.

The daily paper eventually created an intellectual environment. Marshall McLuhan remarked, "People don't actually read newspapers. They get into them every morning like a hot bath." Immersed in this new world of news, people began assuming, by the late nineteenth century, that they *needed*, every morning, something that civilization had existed without for thousands of years — knowledge of what had happened during the previous twenty-four hours across the city, across the country, or later, around the world. Journalism was creating a new human desire: the hunger for fresh stories about current events. This was also the beginning of the mass narrative tradition we live with now, the tradition of both fiction and non-fiction stories created to be shared by large communities of strangers. To read the London *Daily Courant* you did not need to know the editor or visit his printshop; you didn't even need to be in London. You could remain anonymous and yet join this community of readers, giving nothing in return except a modest fee. That was the beginning of the mass public.

Early newspaper publishers, for some decades after the founding of the *Courant*, lived by their wits: they had nothing to sell but facts, ideas, opinions, and the ability to set them down in an orderly way. But as the commercial possibilities of news became evident, those early editor-owners slowly gave way to press barons whose greatest talents were organizational. And in a couple of generations, these new publishers constructed, around their newspapers, great empires of interlocking companies that owned not only newspapers but the presses that printed them, the pulp mills that made the paper, the forests that produced the pulpwood, and sometimes the companies that manufactured the ink. These were prodigious triumphs of industrial organization, but industrialism came at a price: as the newspaper chains and wire services developed their systems of gathering, processing, and exchanging information, the need for efficiency and the doctrine of least cost drove them towards standardization. Articles fell into calcified, predictable patterns, and journalists slowly lost the ability to tell absorbing stories. The everyday style of newspaper writing became constricted and formal; it was often said that the stories the reporters left out of the papers were far more interesting than those they printed.

This style of daily newspaper persisted into the middle of the twentieth century. In 1961, William Weintraub satirized it under the name of the Montreal *Witness* in his novel *Why Rock the Boat?* Weintraub's fictional *Witness* prides itself on publishing stories of massive boredom; it never stoops to be interesting. Weintraub explains that reporters are glamorous people mainly because they withhold their best stories from the public, and the *Witness* journalists manage to withhold just about everything of interest. In private, this makes them "fascinating raconteurs, much sought after for conversation."

Under the system that Weintraub accurately satirized, a newspaper reporter who could tell a story persuasively and directly was a rarity. Even so, over the years a few writers worked out a relationship between journalism and what we now call creative writing. In the nineteenth century, Mark Twain, Stephen Crane, and many lesser figures wrote as both newspaper reporters and novelists. In the 1920s, Ben Hecht moved back and forth between fiction and journalism in Chicago before going off to

Hollywood to help invent the gangster movie and several other forms of mass narrative entertainment.

The great model who emerged around the same time was Ernest Hemingway, who as a young man worked on the *Kansas City Star* and the *Toronto Star*. Many years later, he said that the *Kansas City Star* forced him to learn how to write a simple declarative sentence. When he was there, the newspaper's style book said: "Use short sentences. Use short first paragraphs. Use vigorous English. Be positive, not negative." This was a formula for optimistic Midwestern American journalism, intended to deliver simple information quickly, but Hemingway adapted that style to his own purposes. He carved his own special poetry out of plain words, and he charged his simple declarative sentences with irony, anger, and loneliness. He spent four years working, off and on, for the *Toronto Star*, which sent him to cover the aftermath of war between Greeks and Turks in 1922. One report on the evacuation of refugees ran in the *Toronto Star* under the heading, "A Silent Ghastly Procession Wends Way from Thrace." The article began: "In a never-ending, staggering march, the Christian population of Eastern Thrace is jamming the roads toward Macedonia." He described, with unusual directness, the chaos and misery of refugees.

Hemingway wrote fourteen articles for the *Star* from the Greco-Turkish struggle, and they helped shape him. As newspaper writing, they were excellent; but they became far more potent when he poured them into his fiction. Before he was finished with it, material from that war provided him with three vignettes for his book *In Our Time*, two passages in *Death in the Afternoon*, two crucial flashbacks in his greatest story, "The Snows of Kilimanjaro," part of a lesser-known short story, and the section of *A Farewell to Arms* dealing with the retreat from Caporetto.

Hemingway was asserting his autonomy as a writer within the bland and carefully engineered environment of the newsroom. About the same time, Henry Luce was working on a more institutional response: he and his partner, Britton Hadden, founded *Time* magazine in 1923. Luce became famous for many things, such as unabashedly mixing political opinions with the news; inventing the picture magazine, *Life*; and mangling the English language in pursuit of a vivid, original style. But what made his fortune was the perception that humans see events most clearly (or *believe* they do) when those events are organized as narrative, usually in more or less chronological form.

Luce and Hadden began *Time* magazine as a kind of news summary, a way that people could follow current events without the trouble of working through the deadly columns of thick newspapers. At the start, their resources were pathetic: they had nothing but piles of newspaper clippings, some reference books, and their own imaginations. But they understood narrative as the most persuasive method of organizing an account of reality and understood also that every narrative needs a sense of purpose. Neutrality in storytelling, which newspapers sometimes claimed they were delivering, is probably an impossible goal and in any case is certain to cripple the act of storytelling.

Hadden referred often to Homer's *Iliad* for the vividness of its language, the power of its narrative, and the sense of purpose that gives urgency to the story. Luce, much influenced by his early partner, learned to handle information the way a master sergeant handles soldiers: he and his employees made chaotic facts march in the orderly ranks of narrative, on command. Luce and his colleagues grasped by instinct a central truth of journalism that a few thousand professors later explained in theory — that journalism is an imaginative construction. It follows the rules of its maker as much as it imitates reality.

Time magazine's political influence has disappeared in recent decades, and its storytelling resembles the work in other magazines, partly because everyone else learned so much from *Time*. But at the magazine's peak, a *Time* narrative read like no other. It gave you the news, but not abruptly, like the newspapers, and not obviously. The most carefully machined *Time* story seduced the reader with a slow and highly detailed scene-setting, then a carefully pointed narrative leading towards a conclusion that was intended to convey emotional power. *Time*'s narrative style reached its apogee just before the drastic escalation of the Vietnam War, when its editorial confidence echoed America's political and economic confidence, when the poise of its prose stylists matched the poise of American policy-makers, and when Henry Luce himself was still alive. A 1964 *Time* article about the exchange of spies between the Soviets and the Americans started with this sentence: "One foggy morning in Berlin, a yellow Mercedes from the Soviet zone drew up at the tollgate at the Heerstrasse crossing point." Perhaps *Time* didn't know any more about espionage than the newspapers, but its style made the information dance. A piece on strife in Cyprus started out: "Flowers were in bloom on the crumbling towers of St. Hilarion, and hawks turned soundlessly above Kyrenia." That sentence meant simply that in Cyprus, things don't change a lot. And in the spring of 1964, *Time* ran a cover story on the U.S. ambassador in Saigon, Henry Cabot Lodge, which opened in classic *Time* fashion:

> In the early-morning gloom of Saigon's muggy pre-monsoon season, an alarm clock shrills in the stillness of a second-floor bedroom at 38 Phung Khac Khoan Street. The Brahmin from Boston arises, breakfasts on mango or papaya, sticks a snub-nosed .38-cal. Smith & Wesson revolver into a shoulder holster, and leaves for the office.

Today that sounds less like journalism than like the opening of a popular novel by, say, Tom Clancy — and that's not a coincidence. Just as magazine journalists were imitating novelists, so the novelists heading for the best-seller lists were imitating journalists. These two elements of popular culture were acknowledging their similarities. Around the same period, Arthur Hailey's novels became some of the most successful narratives in the world. Each of them was built on the most exhaustive research into its subject — medicine, banks, the automobile business, or whatever Hailey chose to write about. Sometimes it seemed that the function of characters and story was to animate the research. We could learn about hotels from his novel *Hotel* and about airports from his novel *Airport*, but a couple of months after reading those books it was hard to remember anything about the characters.

Time magazine's carefully calculated approach to the transmission of news stories arose from an understanding of the connection between fiction and reporting, and from the knowledge that journalism can never be a simple, straightforward account of events in the world. It is always a likeness, a semblance, a simulacrum. Journalists function much as artists — good artists and bad artists. We impose on reality the conventions of literary and cinematic art. We transform disparate and often chaotic data into an acceptably organized sequence.

Journalists may occasionally claim they are merely messengers, passing on the facts that come to them, but this pose won't withstand scrutiny. At their most accomplished, journalistic narratives may appear natural and inevitable, as if each story *had* to be told and could not have been told another way. But the facts are chosen and shaped by journalists, and necessarily reflect their interests and traditions. For example, all news media provide far more information about politics than any dispassionate assessment of public interest would dictate; other crucial subjects, most notably science, are by comparison ignored. The reason is that modern journalism descends from the party press of the nineteenth and early twentieth centuries. A few generations ago, newspapers were founded for the clear purpose of setting forth the values of a political party. This created an assumption that politics is the natural subject of journalism — an assumption that continues to reproduce itself. As generation follows generation, reporters start out as political writers, correctly judging that this is the way to success, and when they become editors they know more about politics than any other subject.

A former *Time* magazine reporter, Theodore White, laid one of the foundations of contemporary political journalism when he wrote a book about John Kennedy's campaign, *The Making of the President, 1960*. White obtained access to the inner workings of that campaign, or some of them, and wrote a narrative that embodied the Kennedy approach to politics and White's own understanding of American life in 1960. The book became a best-seller, a textbook for aspiring politicians, and the inspiration for hundreds of other books since. The tradition White founded, of book-length narratives on political campaigns, has taken such firm root in the United States, Canada, and Britain that now there are probably writers who closely imitate White without ever bothering to read him.

At the same time, television news and documentaries were developing visual equivalents of narrative journalism. In making news into narrative, TV leapt ahead of the newspapers — partly because television was anxious to stake its claim as a provider of information and partly because it wasn't burdened by the stale conventions of newspaper writing. At first, TV news was held back by the weight and size of its equipment, but as cameras grew more mobile and tape editing became easier, TV reporters learned how to structure their items as shapely little stories. This, too, was artificial — as artificial as news in print.

A story about the late William Paley, the founder of the CBS network, illustrates the artifice that dominates journalism. One day in 1962, Paley complimented a CBS correspondent, Daniel Schorr, on an interview that Schorr had filmed with an abrasive, insulting East German politician. Paley said: "What impresses me most was how coolly you sat looking at him while he talked to you like that." Schorr was astonished to hear this display of ignorance from his boss. As in most TV interviews, he had been working that day with one camera. The camera filmed the politician while Schorr asked him the questions; then, when that was finished, the camera was moved so that it could film Schorr asking questions or quietly listening. By then, of course, the politician was no longer talking and may even have left the building.

Schorr didn't know how to respond to this compliment, which was no compliment at all. He said, "Mr. Paley . . . surely you know that those were reaction shots, which were done later?" But Paley, the most powerful figure in American broadcasting and the head of the company with the most admired news department, didn't understand this basic fact about how his employees gathered the news. So he asked, "Is that honest?" Schorr (as he recalled later) replied: "That's a funny question. I'm uncomfortable answering it. But no, it's not." So Paley decided it shouldn't be allowed. He ordered that CBS News absolutely prohibit after-the-fact reaction shots. That policy was maintained for a brief period and then forgotten. CBS, like all other broadcasters, went back to the method everyone has always used: piece together little bits of film or tape until they look like reality.

Those who make news into narratives, and those who read or watch or otherwise absorb them, are apparently responding to a human necessity. Mark Turner of the University of Maryland has developed the theory that stories teach us to think. In his book *The Literary Mind*, he argues that telling stories is not a luxury or a pastime but part of developing intelligence. Stories are the building blocks of human thought; they are the way the brain organizes itself. Turner, who works with his university's neuroscience and cognitive-science programs, argues that the mind is essentially literary. Using the neuroscience of Gerald Edelman, he depicts the human mind integrating bits of thought and sensation through overlapping systems, or maps, of neurons. We pull together fragments and find meaning by connecting many elements. And the force that sets the neurons firing and makes these connections possible is narrative — in particular, stories that are blended with other stories. When we compare one story we know with another, we are assembling the elements that make our brains work. Does this account for our *need* to tell stories and listen to them?

George Orwell, perhaps the most admired journalist of this century, left us an account of how narrative arose unbidden in his life, as a force he couldn't entirely control. From about age ten to age twenty-five, the fifteen years up to the point when he became a writer, he conducted what he later called a literary exercise inside himself. He said it was, "The making up of a continuous 'story' about myself, a sort of diary existing only in the mind."

As a child he began imagining himself as Robin Hood or some other hero, but the inner story he told himself eventually grew less heroic and became an almost precise description of what he was actually doing and the things he was seeing. He remembered that for minutes at a time a narrative would run through his head. He gave this example:

> He pushed the door open and entered the room. A yellow beam of sunlight, filtering through the muslin curtains, slanted on to the table, where a matchbox, half open, lay beside the inkpot. With his right hand in his pocket he moved across to the window. Down in the street a tortoise-shell cat was chasing a dead leaf. . . .

And so on. Orwell claimed that for all those years he was making this silent descriptive effort almost against his will, under a kind of compulsion. Perhaps something like this has happened to millions of people, but Orwell's typically honest account is a rare example of a writer exposing this peculiar aspect of his inner life. Orwell developed a highly realistic style, but apparently he was driven by his fantasy life.

He became known as a writer who told the truth even

when it cost him friends, contracts, and for a while, part of his public. He's one of the honoured ancestors of literary journalism, which for many years has been trying to work out the relationship between narrative and reality. Orwell produced several works of literary reporting, but for an understanding of narrative's development the most significant is *The Road to Wigan Pier*. He wrote it on assignment, with great passion and empathy; he inserted himself into the story; and perhaps most surprisingly, he straddled the line between fiction and non-fiction without informing his readers.

In 1936, with the Depression afflicting Britain, Orwell set out to live for a while with workers, including some of the many unemployed, in mining towns like Wigan, near Manchester. He did all the usual research work — interviewed anyone he could, rented rooms with poor families, took part in political discussions, studied reports on housing and health in the library, collected press clippings. He went down in the coal mines three times, which produced some of the most gripping and appalling material: he described the cramped spaces underground as a kind of daily torture chamber for the workers. He spoke of unemployed men scrambling about on gigantic piles of waste to find bits of coal to heat their homes — an exceptionally ignominious and dehumanizing act of thievery for coal miners, whose hard, buried work made European society possible.

At one point, Orwell described the view as he left Wigan: "The train bore me away, through the monstrous scenery of slag-heaps, . . . piled scrap-iron, foul canals, paths of cindery mud. . . . The weather had been horribly cold and everywhere there were mounds of blackened snow."

Journalists are often told not to write of themselves, and for good reason. The public, they are reminded, is not interested in journalists, just in the subjects they are assigned to write about. Nine of ten times, that's good advice, but there are journalists who break that rule with great success. In Orwell's case the story of his own life — the extension, we could say, of that private narrative he carried around with him for fifteen years — became part of his books and articles. He often told his readers about his political development, above all his growing hatred for the Soviet Union and all its friends. And in *The Road to Wigan Pier*, he unleashed his eccentric prejudices against nudists and pacifists, vegetarians and homosexuals, and even people who wore sandals. These remarks, rather than annoying his readers, helped to convince them that they were dealing with a human being rather than the usual journalistic machine; for all their quirkiness, his opinions made his work even more engaging. So that unwritten diary of adolescence and young manhood slowly turned into first-class journalism.

But *The Road to Wigan Pier* raises, in retrospect, an issue that bedevils narrative journalism to this moment: should a writer use only unchanged facts, or can precise information be sacrificed in the service of greater truth? Is it permissible to rearrange the material in artful and perhaps more persuasive ways? Until recently, I was unaware that rearranging for effect was Orwell's practice in *The Road to Wigan Pier*. That passage above, for instance, went on to describe someone Orwell glimpsed from the train, a woman made old before her time by poverty. The look he saw on her face, he remarked, made nonsense of the smug middle-class view that the poor are more or less content with their lot because they have known no other way of life. Orwell wrote, "What I saw in her face was not the ignorant suffering of an animal. She knew well enough what was happening to her — understood as well as I did how dreadful a destiny it was to be kneeling there in the bitter cold, on the slimy stones of a slum backyard."

But as Bernard Crick pointed out in a biography of Orwell, his diaries for that period show that he didn't see her from the train at all. He saw a woman in her position when he was out walking one day, and he shifted her into the train-window scene for reasons of poetic force. And after that passage he inserted a lyrical description of two crows copulating — which also happened not near that train but on another occasion, in another town. Orwell rearranged events to serve his narrative. Crick notes that what Orwell made of his observations was "a very deliberate artistic construction."

So was James Agee's research in America in the same year, 1936. Agee and the photographer Walker Evans went off to spend a month with poor farm families in the rural South, to prepare an article or series for *Fortune* magazine. Agee used the intensely self-conscious strategies of an artist to find the appropriate voice, because he sensed that ordinary magazine narrative would falsify the unrelentingly grim reality of the sharecroppers' lives. He felt he had to step outside journalism and look elsewhere for inspiration, and the voice he developed for that book owed as much to literature and the King James Bible as to modern journalism. *Fortune* magazine didn't use the work that resulted, and when it appeared as a book, *Let Us Now Praise Famous Men*, it was a failure. But twenty years later, republished, it emerged as what it remains today, a classic.

Agee spent two months in the South, one month living with a family of passive, beaten sharecroppers, the Gudgers, whose lives he treated with dignity yet described in the most intense detail. He suffered, like Orwell, from a weighty sense of self, a guilty realization that it might well be impossible to write about the Gudgers without condescension. At the outset, he condemned himself and his colleagues in a great outburst of angry and self-hating hyperbole:

> It seems to me curious, not to say obscene and thoroughly terrifying, that it could occur to an association of human beings drawn together through need and chance and for profit into . . . an organ of journalism, to pry intimately into the lives of an undefended and appallingly damaged group of human beings, an ignorant and helpless rural family, for the purpose of parading the nakedness, disadvantage and humiliation of these lives before another group of human beings, in the name of . . . "honest journalism" (whatever that paradox may mean), of humanity, of social fearlessness, for money, and for a reputation for crusading. . . .

Obviously, Agee could not construct a narrative around the meagre lives of the Gudgers. Their existence was the opposite of a story: it was stasis, the same damn thing every day. So Agee made his personal discovery of the sharecroppers, and his own unfolding responses to this discovery, into the narrative. He spent two pages writing about the floorboards of the Gudgers' house, four pages on their overalls: and he described these details with such precision and poetic force that they became compelling. Like Orwell at Wigan Pier, Agee in the rural South became partly an autobiographer, searching his sophisticated urban consciousness for responses to the narrow desperation of the Gudgers.

Orwell and Agee turned the stories they had uncovered into parables, a common practice for thousands of years. In 1935 in England, the young poet W. H. Auden tried to define this process for his age. He wrote, "There must always be two kinds of art, escape-art . . . and parable-art, that art which shall teach man to unlearn hatred and learn love." Orwell and Agee were trying to make their work into this second kind.

It is the fate of print journalism to keep reinventing the wheel, which in this case means discovering that its strength lies in making sense of the world through story-telling. Orwell and Agee knew that, in their different ways, in the 1930s; but it was necessary for a group of equally self-conscious writers to revive the same impulses and techniques under the name New Journalism in the 1960s and 1970s.

Even that phrase was old. So far as I've been able to

discover, its first appearance was in 1887, when that great critic of culture and civilization, Matthew Arnold, wrote: "We have had opportunities of observing a new journalism which a clever and energetic man has lately invented." Arnold was speaking about W. T. Stead, who edited the *Pall Mall Gazette* in London and used its pages to campaign for child welfare and social progress. Only four years later, someone wrote in the same *Pall Mall Gazette* that Arnold's term "New Journalism," now written with a capital *N* and capital *J*, was already an "abused and much misapplied name."

In the mid-1960s, the term "New Journalism" returned, to cover the work of novelists who wrote about public affairs or crimes — like Truman Capote in his book about a Kansas farm family casually murdered by a couple of drifters, *In Cold Blood*, and Norman Mailer in his book about a protest against the Vietnam War, *Armies of the Night*. At times, these books closely resembled fiction: they reconstructed particularly relevant scenes in the story, they used dialogue, they expressed a point of view. Mailer imported pieces of autobiography; Tom Wolfe, one of the best-known practitioners of this style, though not yet a novelist himself, used status details in the manner of popular novelists like Ian Fleming — he carefully cited brands of liquor, clothing, and cars. Hunter S. Thompson, in *Fear and Loathing on the Campaign Trail*, his book about Richard Nixon's second presidential election in 1972, openly used elements of fantasy, again in the manner of novelists. Wolfe brought together leading examples of the genre in *The New Journalism*, an anthology he edited with

E. W. Johnson. In the introduction, he announced the ascendancy of this form and proclaimed its virtues. Later, Wolfe provided the perfect illustration of his thesis with his best-seller *The Right Stuff*, about the American space program and its roots in the culture of test pilots.

From the beginning, the books and articles of the New Journalists attracted criticism. Often, like urban legends, they sounded too good to be true. Truman Capote insisted that every word of *In Cold Blood* was precisely accurate, but doubters appeared. How could we be sure that so-and-so, now dead, said just those words to so-and-so, now also dead? And in *The Right Stuff*, how could Wolfe understand the unexpressed feelings on a certain occasion of, say, Lyndon Johnson, a man not known for his habit of passing on the details of his inner life? Weren't the events that occurred before Norman Mailer's delighted eyes just a little too convenient, from the standpoint of the storyteller?

And as the years passed, more and more cracks began appearing. John Hersey, who was considered a precursor of the New Journalists for his book *Hiroshima*, wrote a lengthy critique of Wolfe's *The Right Stuff* and concluded that much of it was imagined. Capote's work, too, was increasingly scrutinized, and found to be full of material that could only have been made up by the author. When Wolfe was asked about this sort of criticism, he shrugged it off, as if it didn't matter. On the one hand, the New Journalists preached a doctrine of truth shaped like fiction; on the other, they frequently seemed to acknowledge that the truth was being mixed, from time to time, *with* fiction.

As this controversy was moving along, in fits and starts, narrative journalism was gaining ground. There was a period in the 1980s when *USA Today*, with its brief bites of information, became a model copied by newspapers across North America. More recently, newspapers have been moving towards longer narratives. A turning point was a 1993 report from the American Society of Newspaper Editors called "Ways with Words." It quoted two journalism teachers, who said, "Reporters should incorporate narrative techniques into stories to lead readers through the whole story. Those techniques include actually telling stories, focusing on action, characters and chronology." Other reports followed, along the same lines, making the point (as a journalism professor wrote) that "one of the most marketable things the modern print journalist has to sell, it seems, is coherence." But as a writer, editor, and critic involved in this process for more than thirty years, I now see it as much more complicated than it once seemed. Jon Franklin, a University of Oregon professor who specializes in this kind of writing, summarized the central problem a few years ago in an article for the *American Journalism Review*. "Literary journalism," he wrote, "dramatically increases the level of journalistic responsibilities. Journalists without a keen respect for relationships between fact and truth could impugn the credibility of the whole profession."

The term "New Journalism" has faded, but it affected all of the media and its results can sometimes be embarrassing. In the 1980s, the *Washington Post* had to give back a Pulitzer Prize because the author of the winning piece had invented a heroin-addicted child as the focus of her story. The article, now infamous in journalism history, was called "Jimmy's World" — but Jimmy was an invention, even if the details about his district were accurate. More recently, journalistic narrative has occasionally galloped off into complete fiction. A few years ago, the *Boston Globe* ran a touching and powerful column about two boys, one white and one black, who became friends as patients in a Boston cancer ward; one lived and one died, and in the end the goodness of heart shown by their families proved, perhaps, that the racial wounds of Americans will someday heal. As a newspaper feature it was perfect in every regard but one: not a word of it was true, as researchers discovered when they tried to find the people involved.

The narrative journalism that has developed over recent decades, in television as well as in magazines and newspapers, promises more than the straightforward reporting that journalists of earlier generations were satisfied to practise. But if it is more powerful, it is also more dangerous — and in subtle ways that its most eager practitioners and admirers did not, in the early days, understand. It offers what the Catholic Church calls "an occasion of sin," an invitation to do wrong. In this case, it's an opportunity to mislead. Narrative journalism appears to have no fixed rules except the libel laws, at least in the minds of certain journalists practising it, including some of the most talented. It occurred to me, rather late in this historic development, that just as it requires more talented writers, it also requires more alert and sceptical readers.

It seems clear that narrative presents temptations to the writer that don't exist in the same way with other forms of reporting. Narrative picks up misinformation as a clothes dryer accumulates lint. Bits of rumour cling to it, and so do half-understood anecdotes and casual remarks that may get inflated to the level of fact. The conscience of the writer becomes crucial. Once launched on a narrative, writers may find themselves tempted to improve it, revising reality till it becomes more engaging, more pointed, more memorable. The most sophisticated journalists and documentary filmmakers can become involved in a process that invokes some of the qualities of the urban legend. When reporting fact, we often step dangerously close to fiction.

THE CRACKED MIRROR
OF MODERNITY

ANYONE'S PERSONAL HISTORY as a reader contains certain moments that in retrospect feel like beginnings, openings. When I was twelve or thirteen years old, I picked up an anthology of American short stories and came upon a piece by Ring Lardner called "Haircut." It was then about twenty years old and was considered a classic. Its glow has since faded, and today a reader might find it obvious and overdrawn, like much of Lardner's fiction. But for me, in 1945 or so, "Haircut," just fifteen pages long, was a revelation, a key turning in a lock.

It introduced me to narrative ambiguity, and gave me my earliest glimpses of two subjects large enough to deserve a lifetime's attention: the surprising forms that narrative can take and the energy that writers of the twentieth century have generated through distortions of storytelling. Stories resembling "Haircut" sometimes appeared earlier in literary history, but it is our century that has placed them near the core of literature. And it is also our century that has learned to regard the devious ways of narrative with a certain suspicion, suspicion that reached new intensity with the rise of critical studies in the universities during the last quarter of the century.

"Haircut" concerns the shooting death of an unemployed salesman, Jim Kendall, in a small town in Michigan. The narrator, a barber named Whitey, remembers Kendall with affection. "Jim certainly was a character," Whitey tells us. He also informs us that Jim mistreated his wife and children, bragged about his adulteries, tried to rape a woman who rejected his advances, and liked to play practical jokes on Paul, a young man who was never quite right after a childhood accident damaged his brain.

Whitey speaks indulgently of his late friend Jim: "He was all right at heart, but just bubblin' over with mischief." Whitey describes an elaborate practical joke through which Jim humiliated Julie, the woman he tried to rape. This deeply offended the simple-minded Paul, who idolized Julie. Later, on a duck-hunting expedition, Paul shot and killed Jim.

As he tells us this story, Whitey appears to believe the death was an accident. But we can guess, from the many clues Lardner gives us, that Paul wanted to kill Jim, and that the author considers Paul the agent of justice.

Over seventy-five years or so, "Haircut" has influenced other fiction: Billy Bob Thornton's *Sling Blade*, a much-admired American film of 1996, has characters closely resembling Jim and Paul, a similar dramatic situation, and roughly the same violent resolution. But the main historic interest of "Haircut" lies in the way the barber delivers the story. He's a textbook example of what literary critics call the "unreliable narrator," a phenomenon that was named in 1961 by the critic Wayne Booth in *The Rhetoric of Fiction*.

The unreliable narrator demonstrates how the spirit of the times colours the work of storytellers, and how they in turn help to shape that spirit. We can find unreliable narrators in the books of Agatha Christie and William Faulkner, Vladimir Nabokov and Mordecai Richler — and hundreds of other writers. It's one of the emblematic literary devices of the century.

Civilizations change their collective minds in ways that often aren't discernible until we can look back on them. That's what happened with the unreliable narrator. Beginning around 1900, modernism celebrated or mourned the end of all that was certain, orderly, and purposeful. In literature, modernism turned against the naturalism and realism that dominated the fiction of the nineteenth century. It taught us to look with suspicion on the idea that a straightforward narrative can tell the truth about human life; it began to favour complexity, parody, ambiguity, and ironic self-awareness. In this new atmosphere, the unreliable narrator emerged, the storyteller for the age of relativism, the age of doubt and incredulity. The modern temperament quickens to stories that are splintered in this way: when we read the words of unreliable narrators, we stare into the cracked mirror of modernity.

Sometimes an unreliable narrator withholds crucial

information from the reader; just as often, the narrator doesn't know the facts, or doesn't grasp their meaning. In "Haircut," Whitey holds back none of what he knows. He simply doesn't realize that Jim, the good old boy he's talking about, was a scoundrel. He doesn't understand his own nature, so he cannot see the narrowness and meanness of his outlook. Or, to put it in a context tinged by philosophy, the truth is not present to his consciousness, because the truth is specifically what his consciousness is avoiding. And of course Whitey doesn't understand what effect his words will have on the person he's speaking to — someone relatively sophisticated, like Ring Lardner. Unknowingly, Whitey tells a story of horror and spite and crippled spirits, the American tall tale turned into a nightmare, Mark Twain's amiable small-town jesters transformed into uncaring monsters.

"Haircut" is heavy with irony. Irony demands an element of disparity, and in this case we can't miss the disparity between the way Whitey tells the story and the way we understand what he's saying. It would be pleasant to think that there's no malice here on the author's part, but that notion wouldn't stand much scrutiny. A famous critic of Lardner's day, Gilbert Seldes, wrote: "Lardner has never 'set up' his characters for slaughter. He neither jeers at them nor crows over them." That's what critics always say, or try to say, about satirists we admire and enjoy — and we are almost always wrong to say it. In "Haircut," Lardner appears as an indignant if clever moralist who creates characters and then encourages us to despise them. But he must do it obliquely. A fiction writer and satirist of the nineteenth century, such as Anthony Trollope, would have felt comfortable delivering his own opinions of Whitey directly, in the author's own voice. By the 1920s, however, that kind of moralizing was considered old-fashioned and simple-minded. While readers could look back on an author like Trollope with affection, they could not accept sermonizing from contemporary writers.

When I encountered "Haircut" I realized — I think for the first time in my life — that I was absorbing two accounts of the same events, the fictional narrator's account and the author's. Lardner was speaking to me in a code that his narrator could not understand — but using only the narrator's words. The author and I were in touch, behind the back of the character, colluding against him.

In recent years something resembling that process has been happening, on a vast scale, right across Western culture — but in criticism and scholarship rather than fiction. The sly understanding that Lardner created in my mind has become a common style of thought in the universities across Europe and North America. A set of intellectual strategies has developed into a certain cast of mind, a way of reacting that we might describe as literary exposé. There was a thrill for me, long ago, when I saw through Whitey's evasions in the Lardner story, and a triumph in understanding the truth. A somewhat similar thrill runs through literary criticism today as it looks behind the backs not only of characters in fiction but also of the men and women who wrote significant fiction — and of all those who read them. A few decades ago, a literary critic interested in imperialism might have looked into Jane Austen's books to see how she depicted the rise of the British Empire in her time. But today a critic is much more likely to try to catch Jane Austen in the act of *disguising* the course of empire; today Jane Austen will be brought before the bar of literary history and charged with complicity in the crimes of empire.

Criticism extends some of the grand ideas of the century, and builds on the heritage of great thinkers, notably Marx and Freud. Ideas like Freud's and Marx's seep into our system and stay alive whether we consciously believe them or not — and in fact shape us even if we consciously reject them. Marx taught us, among other things, that even the ideas we think we believe most firmly may be the result of nothing more than false consciousness. Freud taught us to understand that almost anything we think may be a rationalization for thwarted desires. He also taught us that an underground stream runs beneath the surface of life, and that it is in the underground stream that the truth will be found. The hidden tunnel, the buried treasure: these are central metaphors of modernity, the metaphors that helped to place the unreliable narrator in the middle of modern literature. They also helped prepare the way for the wide-ranging collection of ideas and impulses that we now identify under terms such as "postmodern" and "deconstructionist."

Much of this discourse is coloured by the thought of Michel Foucault — including the word "discourse," which he was responsible for inserting into the vocabulary of thousands of intellectuals. Foucault, a genuinely original thinker, saw history where others saw nature; that is, he argued that humans have created much of what seems an obvious and inevitable part of human life, from the concept of madness to the idea of sexuality as central to life. He remains, fifteen years after his death, a breathtakingly audacious thinker who cannot be ignored. But one result of his work was to reduce all of history, including literary history, to conflicts over power. Those who accept Foucault as a major thinker can spend much of their time searching through literature for evidence of oppression. Foucault believed that we are first of all the products of historical forces, and that any form of power — even the most democratic power — is merely a manifestation of war. He wrote: "None of the political struggles, the conflicts waged over power, . . . the alterations in the relations of forces . . . that come about with . . . 'civil peace,' . . . none of these phenomena in a political system should be interpreted except as a continuation of war." The very institutions of learning to which humanity looks for its salvation from oppression were, to Foucault, delusions, part of a scheme for caging all of us. "Power produces knowledge," he wrote. "There is no power relation without the correlative constitution of a field of knowledge, nor any knowledge that does not presuppose and constitute at the same time power relations." Foucault, and many of the scholars he influenced, came to believe that culture itself is politics by other means.

Literature of course has a political dimension, but postmodernism sees it as essentially political; indeed, there is nothing else that is nearly so important about books as their politics. Critics like Fredric Jameson and Stanley Fish, following Foucault, see literature mainly as evidence of oppression. They turn suspicion of power into something resembling paranoia. Look at storytelling this way for a while and all of literary history appears to be a cheat. In fact, contemporary criticism seems to say that the perpetrators of literature have been getting away with something for hundreds of years and must be exposed. Professors and students turn into police officers; the SWAT team of critics arrives on the doorstep of literature and says, in effect, come out with your hands up and your hidden meaning clear. And like a detective, the postmodern critic is happiest when finding the cover-up — when proving, for instance, that you can discover sexism lurking behind the sentimental accounts of women's lives in Charles Dickens. In this kind of criticism, the verdict on the author is usually guilty as charged. Malcolm Bradbury, the British novelist and teacher, said it bluntly: the deconstructionists have proven that literature has been written by entirely the wrong people for entirely the wrong reasons.

There are many principles behind postmodern criticism, but only a single rule that must always apply: when a serious book opens, clouds of muddled thought arise and envelop the reader; it is the critic's duty to banish those clouds so that the sun of intelligence can shine through. The postmodern critic sets out to demystify literature, call it into question, unpack it, interrogate it, deconstruct it. This is not merely an intellectual exercise:

it's an earnest search for the truth that will make us free. Moral fervour runs exuberantly through this field, unrestrained by modesty or insecurity. Critics attack what they consider false values, in the name of what they hope will prove true values. Perhaps the search is more misguided than not, perhaps it only occasionally offers a small nugget of truth. But it is indeed a search. A Canadian critic, Michael Keefer, clearly stated the purpose at the beginning of the 1990s: "Modes of criticism which lay bare the social constraints and power structures which lie behind any act of literary creation or interpretation have an obvious potential as instruments of liberation."

Jacques Derrida, the French philosopher who did as much as anyone to create postmodern thought, teaches that there is no one valid meaning of a literary work — or, as he says, "a text" — because language floats free of an author's intentions and will be interpreted in as many ways as there are readers. The original intention of the author may well be taken into account, but it will be only one of many factors considered when a work of literature is being analyzed or taught.

Postmodern criticism will not be diverted from its duty by considerations of literary value. A writer's use of language, depth of feeling, narrative strength, ingenuity, structure, empathy — these are not necessarily qualities to be admired but are more or less extraneous to the critic's real interest. The theorist asserts theory's right to challenge and expose whatever an author has set down. Postmodernism intends to be anti-authoritarian, yet it often has an authoritarian feeling: to read it is to hear orders being given, papal edicts being read. Certainly that's the effect of Foucault's prose. Postmodern critics are enemies of oppression, of course, but their work can become a kind of oppression, a form of thought control. And there is a strict political line: a left-wing view of society is more or less assumed from the start. This gives a sense of direction and purpose to literary theory, but at the same time it profoundly annoys anyone who does not accept radical views of society. On its worst days, postmodernism reduces literature to a site where various modes of discourse can intersect, and uses writers mainly as examples in support of theories about power relations, society, history, racism, sexism, and so on. At its best, it opens new ways of understanding.

Roland Barthes, perhaps the most brilliant essayist connected with postmodernism, demonstrated that thinking of this kind can generate insights into everything from Greta Garbo to the city of Tokyo. Another great explorer of postmodern territory, Umberto Eco, has a character in his novel *The Name of the Rose* who says: "Books are not made to be believed, but must be subjected to inquiry." That seems reasonable, but postmodernism leads us towards a sometimes outlandish way of looking at narrative and culture.

Modernism in the arts was a rebellion, a multitude of radical ideas, but it did not claim that literature is inherently oppressive; and it believed that its own view of art and life had universal value. Postmodernism, on the other hand, believes that universalist thinking oppresses those who do not accept mainstream values — an idea we tacitly endorse when we say that we have no right to impose our morality on other cultures. Modernism had authority: it was as magisterial in its assumptions as the traditions it opposed. It replaced one set of great artists with another; postmodernism wonders whether a great artist can or should exist, and even wonders if great art exists.

In the most common view of postmodernists, narrative is a deception. The world is not a place of beginnings and endings and middles, a place of coherence — and when narrative arranges the world in that way in order to tell a story and reach out to an audience, narrative lies. If we insist on turning to fiction, it must be entirely self-conscious and must constantly remind us that it is indeed fiction.

Postmodernism has created a tone or mood that was best summed up by Linda Hutcheon of the University of Toronto. As she has put it, postmodernism "takes the form of self-conscious, self-contradictory, self-undermining statement. It is rather like saying something whilst at the same time putting inverted commas around what is being said. . . . Postmodernism's distinctive character lies in this kind of wholesale 'nudging' commitment to doubleness or duplicity."

In those words, she seems to be describing not only a contemporary way of thinking but also certain key books written much earlier in this century, in particular those that use an unreliable narrator. If we consider recent criticism like Hutcheon's alongside certain early modern literary works, striking relationships begin to appear. It is

as if the unreliable narrator had been invented to satisfy
the "self-conscious, self-contradictory, self-undermining"
imagination of postmodernism. The perfect example is *The
Good Soldier* by Ford Madox Ford, which appeared in 1915.

The man who speaks to us in *The Good Soldier* has
been called "the classic unreliable narrator." The story
concerns two affluent married couples, John and Florence
Dowell, who are Americans, and Edward and Leonora
Ashburnham, who are British. The four of them become
friends early in this century as they enjoy a more or less
permanent holiday at German spas and French Riviera
hotels. These are people of privilege, and one of their
privileges is a casual amorality, but that's not what cen-
trally concerns Ford Madox Ford. His novel, an
enthrallingly readable piece of storytelling, is also an
exploration of knowledge: between the lines, and now
and then in the lines themselves, *The Good Soldier* asks difficult questions. How much of what matters to us can we
really know? How can we learn it? Are we limited to a
narrow and mistaken view of reality by who we are?

The story of *The Good Soldier* involves adultery, elaborate deceptions, two suicides, someone who goes
permanently insane, and intimations of incest; but these
events, even the two deaths, mainly occur offstage, in a
way that makes them almost incidental. That's because
the real action of *The Good Soldier* takes place within the
mind of John Dowell, the narrator. What makes the novel
an essential document of modern life is the picture of
John's mind groping towards knowledge. He knows less
about what's happening than any of the others — for

instance, he believes that his own marriage has remained unconsummated because his wife has a heart condition, when in fact she does not; and he has no idea that she is Edward Ashburnham's lover. Perhaps John understands himself least of all; certainly he seems entirely to miss the homosexual side of his feeling for Edward. John, in truth, is a bit of a ninny, and hardly seems to know when he contradicts himself. At the beginning he deludes us even as he deludes himself, and soon we learn not to trust him. He begins the book by saying:

> This is the saddest story I have ever heard. We had known the Ashburnhams for nine seasons of the town of Nauheim with an extreme intimacy — or, rather, with an acquaintanceship as loose and easy and yet as close as a good glove's with your hand. My wife and I knew Captain and Mrs. Ashburnham as well as it was possible to know anybody, and yet, in another sense, we knew nothing at all about them.

So on the one hand, he assures us the two couples were intimate friends; and on the other, he tells us they were not. And even as he delivers this self-cancelling account of their relationship, he lies. Because (as we will eventually discover) one of the Dowells, Florence, knew a good deal about one of the Ashburnhams, Edward. And of course this ignorance, this failure of comprehension, is the reason the author made John the narrator; it is the reason *The Good Soldier* evokes the modern temperament at its most baffled.

By using John to speak to us, Ford raises self-doubt to the level of literary style. And gradually we come to realize that we are looking at something larger than private self-doubt. It's the doubt of European civilization that Ford is addressing. John Dowell acknowledges that we may be wondering why he has written all this. He says it's common for those who have witnessed some disaster, like the sack of a city or the destruction of a whole people, to set down what they have seen for the benefit of others — for, as he says, "generations infinitely remote."

There are many hints like that in the book: Ford's purpose is the invention of a new form of narrative for a new historic period. The old narrative technique, of the eighteenth and nineteenth centuries, was appropriate for a more self-confident world, in which certain truths were held in common; but in the world Ford inhabited, the world most of us now inhabit, those truths have been questioned or discarded. When John tells us he has no way of knowing what his story means, he is in a sense speaking for European civilization, which at the moment of the book's appearance — 1915 — was tearing itself to pieces in an all-devouring war.

The Good Soldier announced a new era in storytelling, an era in which the classical form of irony would become a central element, sometimes even *the* central element. *The Good Soldier* is among the ancestors of all those novels and TV programs in which the writers use irony as if there were no other way to see the world. Even the title carries irony — Capt. Edward Ashburnham, while he holds a British army commission, isn't much of a soldier and certainly isn't good. Perhaps the title also covers the narrator, John, who is a "good soldier" in the sense that he keeps his head down, asks few questions, and puts up with almost anything done to him; he's like a conscript in an army run by idiots, but he trudges onward anyway, fighting a war he doesn't understand for a reason he can't give.

While John Dowell exists on one of the higher rungs of literature, the unreliable narrator also lives a comfortable life in popular fiction. He made his most famous appearance in 1926 as Dr. James Sheppard, the narrator of *The Murder of Roger Ackroyd*, the most discussed of the forty-two books in which Agatha Christie used her Belgian sleuth, Hercule Poirot. It was also her most subversive book, because it threw a cloud of suspicion over one of the major character types on which popular English fiction depended — the same character type that was to populate much of Christie's fiction for several decades to come.

It was at this moment that Agatha Christie adopted the approach of twentieth-century literature, even if only in a mechanical way, and joined with all those forces that were undermining through literature the conventions of rational self-confidence on which culture had based itself since the eighteenth century. Christie methodically betrayed the expectations of her readers and found her own expression of the Freudian idea that turned out to be the century's principal slogan, the idea that can be paraphrased as "Things are never what they seem."

The unreliable narrator of *The Murder of Roger Ackroyd*

appears for most of the book to be supremely reliable. If we understand this novel as an exploration of a murderer's twisted mind, we do so only retroactively. He's no John Dowell, whose contradictions glare at us from the first paragraph. Dr. Sheppard is apparently an honest general practitioner who lives with his sister Caroline in a village called King's Abbot. His tone suggests that he's one of those sensible, quietly genial Englishmen, skilful at what he does, much put upon by silly people but tolerant of those who lack his own good sense. He finds his sister's tendency to gossip a particular trial, but he does his best to keep from disclosing to her the more sensitive information about his patients.

Dr. Sheppard tells us about a local woman, Mrs. Ferrars, whose husband died not long ago and who has herself just died suddenly. He describes her friend Roger Ackroyd, the rich man in the village, owner of a grand house. Roger Ackroyd is murdered, and Dr. Sheppard tells us the details, omitting only a few. These few, however, are crucial: it's Dr. Sheppard who has been blackmailing Mrs. Ferrars, because he knows she poisoned her cruel husband; and it's Dr. Sheppard who murdered Ackroyd when Ackroyd was about to learn the truth. Dr. Sheppard doesn't directly lie to us; he simply omits the most damning information.

But a certain Hercule Poirot has moved in next door. He and Dr. Sheppard investigate various suspects — Ackroyd's step-son, a stranger who has been glimpsed near the house, even the butler and the maid. And then, nine pages before the end of this 306-page book, Poirot accuses

Dr. Sheppard of the murder. He offers him a chance to commit suicide, so the doctor spends a night writing his account of the case and then, we are led to believe, takes a fatal dose of poison, his honour and his family's good name preserved.

The Murder of Roger Ackroyd is perhaps the most playful of Christie's books. It's also the one most frequently discussed by critics, who themselves sometimes turn playful in response. In 1998 Pierre Bayard, a Paris critic who has written on literary lies as they appear in Guy de Maupassant and Marcel Proust, brought out a remarkable book, *Qui a tué Roger Ackroyd?* (Who Killed Roger Ackroyd?). This is a work of postmodernism at play. It extends Christie's trick to another level by trying to show that Roger Ackroyd was in fact murdered by Hercule Poirot himself; apparently Poirot was cagier than we have ever suspected. Bayard, using only the facts given in the book, reasons that Poirot convinced Dr. Sheppard of his guilt and persuaded him, through some sort of subliminal suggestion, to write his confessional memoir and commit suicide. Bayard thus makes Dr. Sheppard doubly unreliable — first of all when he failed to tell us he was the killer, and then again when he told us he was.

We find unreliable narrators strewn across the literature of the century, often in novels regarded as central to the literary imagination of their time. In 1925, F. Scott Fitzgerald told *The Great Gatsby* through the eyes of Nick Carraway, an onlooker and occasional participant who finds the story he's telling hard to understand. Nick doesn't lie to us, but he moves, in the course of the novel, from easygoing ignorance towards a sketchy understanding of the attractive but thoughtless and selfish people who dominate the story. In *The Sound and the Fury* by William Faulkner, published four years later, the role of unreliable narrator splits into three voices, the three Compson brothers, who tell the story of their sister Caddy and her hasty, loveless marriage. The first brother, Benji, is severely retarded and entirely unable to know what has happened — which partly explains the use in the title of the quotation from *Macbeth*: "Life's . . . a tale / Told by an idiot, full of sound and fury, / Signifying nothing." The second brother, Quentin, is clever, but he's blinded by fantasies of family honour and incestuous feelings for his sister. And the third brother, Jason, is a thief and a liar.

More recently, Kazuo Ishiguro, in *The Remains of the Day*, makes the butler in a grand English house his unreliable narrator. Stevens, the character played in the film by Anthony Hopkins, writes a smug and defensive prose, obviously his idea of how a man of dignity should express himself. Stevens has no idea that he's a snob, no idea that he's emotionally entombed, and no idea that there can be anything wrong in his devoted and unquestioning service to his master. At some point, we realize that the subject of the novel is the consciousness of Stevens. Ishiguro wants us to see that Stevens has missed his only chance for a rich emotional life and squandered his career in the service of a man who was a Nazi sympathizer. As we watch, Stevens comes to understand some of this too.

An unreliable narrator speaks to us in *Barney's Version*,

the 1997 novel that is among the triumphs of Mordecai Richler's career. Barney Panofsky, the self-hating film producer who sets down what he calls "the true story of my wasted life," does not lack understanding of his nature and his situation. He's unreliable for a more touching reason: Alzheimer's disease is gnawing at his mind, nipping away pieces of his memory, eliminating a few words here and there, then perhaps a crucial scene or two. He makes many mistakes, and the book comes to us with footnotes and an afterword by his pedantic son, Michael Panofsky. Barney slips into oblivion before Michael discovers that in the most horrifying event of his life, the murder he was accused of committing, Barney for once was a reliable narrator who told nothing less than the truth.

A life such as Barney's can be made to matter only through the fresh use of various familiar narrative patterns. That's the narrative tradition's great power: the ability to bestow meaning on otherwise disorganized events. Doris Lessing, the novelist, remarked at a conference in 1998: "We value narrative because the pattern is in our brain. Our brains are patterned for storytelling, for the consecutive." But she argued, in criticizing contemporary mass culture, that the pattern is being broken up, that much of culture now comes to us in hurried bits and pieces, whether in books, films, or TV shows. She saw around her the collapse of traditional narrative, the kind she grew up on and still regards as fundamental to civilized life. At that same conference, a New York professor of literature, Morris Dickstein, argued with her, as

follows: "The fact is that the whole world has speeded up
. . . and there's no reason . . . why the media and literature,
which to some degree reflect the pace of life in the world,
should not also have speeded up."

Dickstein seemed to think Lessing's views were based
on nothing better than nostalgia. He admitted that it may
be hard for some of us to adjust, but he pointed out that
since the earliest days of modern literature there have
been complaints about discontinuity; he cited James
Joyce's *Ulysses* as an example of a book widely condemned for that reason. Now *Ulysses* has been installed in
the great tradition of literature. The old pre-modern narratives, he said, do "not really reflect the rhythm of life as
we experience it in the twentieth century."

This is a dispute that arises wherever the word "narrative" is raised today. It seems to me that in this case
both sides are right and both are wrong. Lessing is right
that we cannot do without narrative, but wrong, I think,
to believe it is vanishing from the world around us; Dickstein is right to say the form of narrative constantly
changes, but wrong to suggest that traditional narrative
has lost credibility. After Dickstein spoke, Doris Lessing
said she knew that if she mentioned narrative she would
be in trouble. That was her rueful way of acknowledging
the enormous power that postmodern thought has
achieved in recent times: she felt that stating one of her
most cherished beliefs, something she has lived with inti-
mately for fifty or sixty years, was a little dangerous and
maybe a little old-fashioned. She was right. Today it is
a rare academic critic who will say a kind word for

straightforward narrative; and even among literary journalists, praise for an old-fashioned "good read" is now
routinely delivered in rather sheepish and apologetic
terms, as if one were defending royalty or the taking of
snuff.

The enemies of postmodernism love to say its theories
are beginning to go out of fashion, but that wishful thinking collapses if we look at literary journals, university
publishing, or university curricula. During the last thirty
years, these ideas have won legitimacy throughout much
of literate society. Their influence turns up far beyond the
universities where it is concentrated.

Having become securely lodged in the universities,
postmodernism seems at times to reverse what many
imagined was the university's function. Where once we
might have asked professors to make difficult writers
easy for us, now they make easy writers difficult, turning
them into puzzles, muffling them in layers of aggres-
sively impenetrable jargon and priestly theory. There is
no work of literature that cannot be made more obscure
by postmodern critics. What starts out as storytelling
becomes, in their hands, a kind of elaborate cultural
dance, whose choreography can be understood only by
critics and teachers.

How is a critic to deal with postmodernists? Warily,
sceptically, yet with intense curiosity. Their outrageous
assumptions, their absurd demands, have the virtue of
breathing life into the debate over culture, and their professors have acquired a certain charm. I love them for
their awkward anger, and I love them for their conviction

that much is at stake in the study of literature — a conviction that was fading until they came along. I love the way they do narrative the honour of distrusting and challenging it. I love their arrogance, but wish they could not so easily teach it to their students. And I love their sense of mission. The postmodern critic imagines that most of us are enraptured and baffled by literature, locked in the castle of our ignorance like innocent maidens bewitched by evil sorcerers, awaiting princely deliverance.

Even if that's no more than a fairy tale, the postmodern critics are not always wrong when they ask us to treat literature as a puzzle. There's a passage in *The Book of Evidence*, a novel by John Banville, that throws light on one corner of this question. Banville's narrator is not only unreliable but also apparently mad — and a murderer as well. But out of his insanity, if that's what it is, he produces a fresh and piercing comment on the reading of narrative. He apparently doesn't much like unreliable narrators; they leave him edgy and uncertain. He says:

> If I was reading something . . . and agreeing with it enthusiastically, and then I discovered at the end that I had misunderstood entirely what the writer was saying, had in fact got the whole thing arse-ways, I would be compelled at once to execute a somersault, quick as a flash, and tell myself, I mean my other self, that stern interior sergeant, that what was being said was true, that I had never really thought otherwise. . . .

Perhaps that's madness speaking — and yet, it seems likely to me that something of that kind has occasionally been experienced by all but the most learned or the most obtuse of readers. Certainly it happens to me. It's the private shame of being found out by oneself, followed by the secretly renewed knowledge that we are not as bright as we thought we were.

A book that could well have induced this feeling in Banville's madman is *Pale Fire* by Vladimir Nabokov, a novel that brings together many of the great issues raised by storytelling through our century. In his masterpiece of unreliable narration, Nabokov pushes against the limits of storytelling and manipulates the reader as cheerfully and imaginatively as he manipulates the narrator. Nabokov once said, "You can get nearer and nearer . . . to reality; but you never get near enough because reality is an infinite succession of steps, levels of perception, false bottoms, and hence . . . unattainable." He was summarizing one of the conundrums of existence in a time when most of us, having abandoned the explanations of orthodox religions, have found it necessary to carve out, somehow, a personal understanding of the world. *Pale Fire*, a highly questionable tale told by a highly suspicious character, is Nabokov's most relentless attempt to reach through all those layers of mystery.

Pale Fire has been puzzling readers since it appeared in 1962. Perhaps its initial appeal lies in a supreme demonstration of a great novelist's virtuosity, but as we come to know it we understand that much more is at stake. It's a book that encourages us to contemplate, in scores of oblique and unexpected ways, questions of identity, memory, and historic vision, all key problems in storytelling; and we are also asked to observe in detail the anxiety of a narrator who has a story he must urgently tell though even he sometimes seems to doubt its reliability.

Nabokov readers rightly anticipate that we will have the pleasure of uncovering many aspects of the story for ourselves. He pays us the tribute of assuming that we can follow his clues where they lead us and — perhaps — satisfy ourselves about the story's meaning. When I first read this book as a reviewer in the 1960s, I felt much as I did when reading Ring Lardner's "Haircut" in adolescence. I experienced again the sense that the writer and I were talking behind the narrator's back. Nabokov makes that experience into a highly adult form of play.

Pale Fire unfolds like the landscape in an alien country. When Nabokov sent the manuscript to his publisher, he wrote a note to accompany it: "I trust you will plunge into the book as into a blue ice hole, gasp, re-plunge, and then . . . emerge and sleigh home, metaphorically, feeling the tingling and delightful warmth reach you on the way from my strategically placed bonfires." In those words, Nabokov was addressing everyone who reads the book.

Pale Fire, like many of Nabokov's books, concerns an identity crisis, or a series of identity crises. We can understand why he so often chose this theme. To a spectacular degree, Nabokov lived out the characteristic dislocations of the twentieth century. The communists in Russia robbed him of his native culture, after which he moved to Berlin and re-established himself, only to be robbed of a future in Germany by the Nazis. Eventually he settled in the United States and learned to write the English of a master — and all along, as this was happening, he was pouring elements of his life into the narratives he was writing. He passed along some of his most poetic reactions to dislocation in *Speak, Memory*, one of the great autobiographies of the century. Other observations he conveyed indirectly through his fiction — for instance, his fascination with the highway culture of his adopted America colours the pages of *Lolita*, his most popular book. In many other books he led his readers through the special uncertainties of immigrants, adrift in new worlds, threatened by failure, loneliness, and poverty, threatened even by madness if they cannot accept calmly the radical change that is their fate.

In dealing with these subjects, the unreliable narrator offers an array of possibilities, and Nabokov ingeniously exploits them in *Pale Fire*. His story takes place, to the extent that it takes place anywhere, in a college town that resembles Ithaca, New York, where Nabokov taught at Cornell University. We are led to understand that a poet who lived there, John Shade, has been murdered and has left behind a poem of 999 lines, whose affecting climax is the suicide by drowning of his daughter. Charles Kinbote, a scholar who knew John Shade, has written a commentary to the poem and many footnotes, plus an index, and together these tell the story. Here the unreliability of the narrator Kinbote is the novel's very method.

The most obvious irony appears in the disparity between Kinbote's view of his place in the university community and the way we readers understand it. He sees himself as the close friend of the dead poet, John Shade, but we realize that Shade merely tolerated him, perhaps out of kindness. Here Nabokov describes, without self-pity, feelings he must have endured in America — a man of some eminence, reduced to a figure many people find eccentric and marginal and even, perhaps, because of his accent when speaking English, comic. But more than all that, we realize fairly soon that Kinbote is not only unreliable, he's insane.

Kinbote wants to persuade us that the Shade poem is not in fact about Shade's daughter but concerns events in the far-off northern kingdom of Zembla, Kinbote's homeland. And eventually Kinbote slyly informs us of what he considers the "real story" here — that he is himself the deposed king of Zembla, Charles the Beloved, living in disguise in America as a humble professor. Furthermore, he wants us to know, Shade's murder was a mistake: the killer was an assassin sent by Zembla to kill Kinbote, who happened to be walking beside Shade at the time of the shooting.

Even as Nabokov lets us understand how dubious the story is, and points out the deficiencies in the narration, he uses old-fashioned methods of suspense. Nabokov wants to have it both ways: he'll discount Kinbote's story while at the same time asking us for that "willing suspension of disbelief" that Coleridge once named as a necessity in the reading of stories. Miraculously, Nabokov carries it off, in some cases by using the standard machinery of suspense films and novels, such as cutting back and forth between Charles Kinbote and the journey of the assassin sent by Zemblan radicals to eliminate him. And of course, just like the writer of a thriller, Nabokov prolongs the suspense as long as he can.

Here the communications from writer to reader behind the narrator's back are flowing swiftly: Nabokov is telling us that Kinbote is mad, with the particular madness of the forced expatriate. Kinbote has been so overcome by the trauma of expatriation and resettlement that he has reimagined and flagrantly romanticized his entire life. But there's another level of unreliability: Nabokov seems to suggest that John Shade himself has written the commentary, as well as the poem. And at a further level, it appears possible that Kinbote and his story have all been created by a mad Russian exile bearing the name V. Botkin.

At the end, the actual author, Nabokov, has told a story of great tenderness and understanding in a way that no one ever told a story before. He has taken us to emotional places we might never have visited otherwise, and led us through mazes of meaning that can only be instructive. He has shown us one more way narrative heightens our understanding of the world around us — a way as rewarding as it is complex.

Pale Fire improves with age; it demonstrates that of all the writers who tried to find new ways of storytelling in this century, no one understood the infinite resources of narrative better than Vladimir Nabokov. And in recent years, changing steadily as all great books do, it has acquired a new charm: it seems to have been written in the full knowledge of how literature and narrative would be seen at the end of the century in postmodern criticism, most of which had not been imagined when Nabokov sat down to write his masterwork.

NOSTALGIA, KNIGHTHOOD, AND THE CIRCLE OF DREAMS

WHEN LEONARDO DICAPRIO stands at the prow of the *Titanic* and shouts ecstatically into the wind, "I'm the king of the world!" he's already won the audience's collective heart by playing a role that's been familiar to most of us since childhood. His character, Jack Dawson, is the hero of what was once routinely called a romance. Critics used that term to distinguish this sentimental and more or less preordained form of storytelling from other forms; we rarely need it now, because the romance has grown so popular that the word covers nearly everything in mass culture except outright comedy. Note that before he stands on that prow, Jack Dawson has already acted out a key element in romance: his physical beauty, his eloquence, and the nobility of his spirit have won the heart of a well-born lady who would normally be forbidden to him; he has thus leapt upward about six social classes in one seduction, an achievement rooted in the history of narrative. And before the story ends, as hero and heroine float on the cold, dark waters of the Atlantic, Jack will demonstrate his nobility by calmly accepting his own death and giving up his life for this same lady fair, asking only that for the sake of their love she never give up on life. That final speech, which provoked tears from millions of viewers in 1997, was already familiar in essence to playgoers and novel-readers a century before.

Those who enjoy the narratives of mass culture — that is to say, billions of us — choose what we will read or see by standards that embody unresolved contradictions. We in the mass audience require characters who surprise us, but we also want their feelings to resemble our own — after all, that's what we mean when we call a character human. We demand originality, but we don't much like anything that catches us entirely unawares. An architect I used to know complained that when people hired him, they made it clear that they loved to be innovative but didn't want to do anything for the first time. We're like that. As an audience we accept strange and exotic settings, yet we want to feel comfortable as soon as a story takes us there. Characters can live in other centuries or visit distant galaxies, but we want them to laugh at the same jokes we enjoy. Above all, we require that plots be made the way we think plots have always been made, with heroes and heroines, and villains, and a side we can take.

Our tastes can be frustrating to artists who hope for success in the mass media, but there seems no way to change us. We can paraphrase Walt Whitman and say that if you accuse us of inconsistency, so be it: we don't just contain multitudes, as he claimed to do, we *are* multitudes. And because a mixture of novelty and familiarity is what we so clearly want, narratives produced for mass culture often seem nostalgic even as they come spanking new from the factory.

In one sense, the history of mass storytelling runs in a straight line, a progress from technical invention to technical invention — first novels, then films, then radio, then television, and recently the Internet. But that describes only the media and the industries that make the media possible. If we ignore the technology for a moment and consider the stories and themes, mass culture appears to circle endlessly around the same trail, meeting on its path again and again the same characters in roughly the same stories. It is a good general rule that the more successful a work of mass culture, the more it will conform to a pattern with which our grandparents were on intimate terms.

So when Jack Dawson bravely says farewell to his love in *Titanic,* no one, not the meanest cynic, not even a critical moviegoer who has been watching this film in angry boredom and disgust — no one will find Jack's decision even slightly surprising or doubt for a moment that what he does is, given the conventions governing his life and ours, just and right.

After all, everyone in the audience, male or female, has done much the same thing. Or rather, we imagine we would, under the appropriate circumstances; certainly we have done something like that in our dreams, because the same tradition of fantasy and heroism that dictates

Jack's actions also lies beneath our dreams. Eileen Whit-field, at the end of her biography of Mary Pickford, reminds us: "Film and its cousin in the field of moving images — television — dominate our lives. They have affected how we think about ourselves, how we filter our reality, and how we dream."

If a story like Jack's appears in our dreams, it's because something very like it has been told, with infinite variations, over and over again, by good artists and bad, on land and sea, in the forests of England and the deserts of America and the rice fields of Japan, in books or films or television, since . . . well, since the year 1819. Of all the dates we can choose as the founding year of mass story-telling, 1819 has the best claim. When we search for the origins of the themes that run persistently through the stories we tell and listen to, we sometimes find that they recede endlessly into the past, their sources growing ever more dim and obscure. But in the vast region of our cultural geography dominated by romance, the road signs are clear. They all point to Edinburgh, where in 1819 Sir Walter Scott brought out his most influential novel, *Ivanhoe*.

That book's characters and attitudes and situations have come tumbling down the generations to the film *Titanic* and to many thousands of other resting places. Scott, in *Ivanhoe*, gave the romance the form it has taken ever since. At the same time, he opened up a way of see-ing manhood, heroism, and society, with results that shaped history as well as culture. We cannot say that all popular narrative comes from Scott; we can say that a line traced from his work to the present moment shows one of the significant ways that storytelling developed in his century and ours.

The cowboy gunman of the Old West, a central figure in the mass imagination for much of this century, was one clear descendant of the knights who populated *Ivanhoe* and other books by Scott. The cowboy followed a code of conduct that Scott laid down, and by the middle of this century, more than 125 years after *Ivanhoe*'s appearance, much of the world understood that code. We also understood that those who lived by it were the true gentlemen, and that their souls were pure despite their rough exteriors. In 1946, when I saw one of the great John Ford films, *My Darling Clementine*, I already knew — at age fourteen — why it was that the gunmen, Henry Fonda as Wyatt Earp and Victor Mature as Doc Holliday, treated ladies with great delicacy, as if they were china dolls that would break under the slightest pressure; I knew why the same gunmen assumed that loyalty was more important than almost anything else in the world; and I understood that they would not take advantage of the weak or treat even their enemies unfairly. All this emotional land had been cleared for me by the stories and films of childhood, most of them influenced by Sir Walter Scott. I was also ready to be told, as *My Darling Clementine* told me, that these noble gunfighters were on the side of good, and their enemies, the Clantons, whom they would conquer in the gunfight at the O.K. Corral, were profoundly and irredeemably evil. This format, this armature of emotion and morality, was given to John Ford, to me, and to everyone else who loved westerns by the traditions Scott passed down to us. It was given also, by extension, to Akira Kurosawa, the great Japanese director, who acknowledged that he learned much about heroic movies by studying John Ford. Kurosawa's films, such as *The Seven Samurai*, imported a version of this code into Japan, married it to ancient Japanese tradition, and made samurai movies and TV programs as vital in Japan as the western was in the United States. *The Seven Samurai* was then converted back into the American idiom, as a popular film and a TV series, *The Magnificent Seven*.

Hollywood celebrated another version of medieval knighthood when it embraced the private investigator in the form of Humphrey Bogart as Sam Spade in *The Maltese Falcon* or Robert Mitchum as Philip Marlowe in *Farewell, My Lovely*. Bravely walking the mean streets of America, the private eye is all on his own, like a Scott hero, and with his lonely courage he often faces down corrupt power, again like a Scott hero; even under the worst pressure, he maintains his belief in a professional code, knowing that if all else goes wrong, he will still have lived on a higher moral plane than those with whom he dealt. In more recent times the cowboy has largely vanished from the popular imagination, and the private eye was first joined and then overtaken on television by the independent-minded police detective, on programs like "NYPD Blue." On the surface, this figure may seem an unlikely product of the tradition Scott propagated; two decades ago, we might not have accepted a free-spirited knight errant who was also a government employee with a civil-service pension. And something else would have been startling: this particular knight works beside women who have status equal to his and are just as likely to save him as he is to save them, which requires an ingenious sorting-out of male-female relationships. Feminism prepared the ground for the new role given women, and the fictional police detectives owe much of their independence to a cultural shift brought about by a generation of anti-establishment, anti-authority rhetoric. The sceptical way we now speak of institutions has made it possible to imagine heroic figures fighting for truth and justice within politically influenced bureaucracies. The heroes struggle against arbitrary power that — just as in *Ivanhoe* — demands their loyalty but does not always deserve it.

Another version of the same figure appears in space fiction, perhaps most notably in the form of Han Solo, the freelance spaceship jockey played by Harrison Ford in the original *Star Wars* in 1977. Like many heroes encountered in romances, particularly westerns, Solo begins as something of a cynic and then finds his idealistic spirit aroused by a noble cause. *Star Wars* also adhered to the original style with Princess Leia (Carrie Fisher), a maiden who needs assistance from virtuous young men.

The makers of all these stories borrow elements from the narrative traditions of the whole world, but Scott, more than anyone else, gave these tales their structure. Today he's not much read, and the great majority of those who live in his shadow are at best dimly aware of his significance; many have barely heard of him. Yet he stands behind narrative mass culture, its founder and its inspiration, for better or worse. He's an unlikely figure for this role. After all, his reputation, as it receded into history, acquired a certain stiffness, a patina of formality. His knighthood and his connections to the ideals of Scotland, not to mention the gigantic memorial statue of him in Edinburgh, have created an aura of dignified officialdom. The professors who now study his works and republish them in textually corrected and carefully annotated editions have heightened that impression. But the truth is that Sir Walter Scott was the Steven Spielberg of his time, and more than that.

He has had more influence around the world than any other British writer except Shakespeare. In the nineteenth century, Wilkie Collins, a popular master of the melodramatic novel, called Scott "the Prince, the King, the Emperor, the God Almighty of novelists." George Eliot said she hated hearing a word said against him, and a modern critic, Walter Allen, has said that Scott "made the European novel." Today we still live in a world flavoured and scented by Scott's imagination; the romantic era, as he expressed it, has in a sense never ended. Its rules of storytelling remain our rules. Even though we bend them and satirize them, even though we adapt them to feminist themes or other modern purposes, even though we may groan over their predictability, we seem always to return to them.

Scott had a peculiar relationship with history and time. As a writer he looked backward as far as the Middle Ages and as an influence he reached forward at least to our period and likely much farther. He's been described as the last minstrel and the first best-seller — minstrel because in his poetry and his interests he reflected the qualities of the ancient Border ballads, and called one of his poems *The Lay of the Last Minstrel*; best-seller because he wrote the first novels to achieve vast international popularity and inaugurated traditions that yielded best-sellers for many other writers.

Scott came of age with the romantic movement, late in the eighteenth century; he was almost the exact contemporary of Beethoven, Wordsworth, and Coleridge. In his youth a wave of articulated emotion was rising across Europe, a reaction against the rationalism of the Enlightenment. Scott packaged the impulses of the romantic movement for the market — a market that hardly existed until his books brought it into being.

His *Waverley* stories, about early eighteenth-century Scotland, were something new in the world: historical novels. By inventing this form, Scott laid the path for Dumas with *The Three Musketeers*, Victor Hugo with *Les Misérables*, and a multitude of their followers. This was a wonderful new literary device, a means of imaginatively dissolving the passage of time; Scott gave readers something narrative had never before provided, a way to slip out of the narrow provincialism imposed by one's own period and catch at least a little of the feeling of what it was to live in another era. He provided a way to depict politics, and the great movements of history, in personal terms. He introduced the then-radical (and still-questionable) notion that people who lived long in the past, feared their monarchs and their priests, wore different clothes, ate different foods, and usually didn't know what year it was — that these distant people of pre-modern Europe felt, thought, and talked much as we do. This was the idea that launched a literary style that flourishes to this moment. Only about forty years later, Jules Verne decided to work Scott's process in reverse and invent stories of the future using many of the same rules for what we now call science fiction.

Having accomplished all this with the *Waverley* novels, having established himself as a great figure, Scott wrote *Ivanhoe* and sent even more powerful tremors through literature. *Ivanhoe* took him out of Scotland, south to England, and farther back into history — to the twelfth century, the time of the Third Crusade, the summer of 1194. That in itself reflected the taste of the romantic age. A few decades earlier, Voltaire and other Enlightenment thinkers had judged the Middle Ages a distinctly unhappy moment in history, never to be repeated and certainly not to be admired. In reaction, the romantic era began reimagining the Middle Ages, endowing them with simpler virtues and more powerful emotions. The idea arose that humanity in those days was unsophisticated and unspoiled, more vital and authentic. If the Enlightenment considered the Middle Ages a nightmare, the romantics decided they were a splendid dream.

This was the emotional foundation for *Ivanhoe*, and explained its appeal. That book has since been so imitated and parodied, and its plot points so often borrowed, that it almost feels like a work of plagiarism when you read it today. Certainly it contains little that's unfamiliar. It begins:

> In that pleasant district of merry England which is watered
> by the River Don, there extended in ancient times a large
> forest, covering the greater part of the beautiful hills and
> valleys which lie between Sheffield and the pleasant town
> of Doncaster. . . . Here . . . flourished . . . those bands of gal-
> lant outlaws whose deeds have been rendered so popular
> in English song.

The words "merry England," on his first page, evoke
an attitude that was entirely unrelated to documented
fact but nevertheless helped to shape ideas about the English past for generations. The rest of his book evoked a
world that many millions of us were to enter in childhood. Scott placed his story in the time of Richard the
Lion-Heart, his usurper brother, Prince John, and Robin
Hood — all of them background members of the cast.

Wilfred, knight of Ivanhoe, son of Cedric the Saxon,
returns home from the Crusade to claim his love,
Rowena, his father's ward. His father, however, believes
she should marry Athelstane, who has royal Saxon blood,
to help restore the Saxons to power. Ivanhoe also becomes
involved with a beautiful Jewish healer, Rebecca, perhaps
the book's most interesting character. Scott takes us to a
tournament featuring elaborate pageantry and much
bloody jousting. All of this is played out before a society
dominated by knighthood and the code of chivalry, with
its obligations of valour, chastity, honour, and loyalty.
Scott relied heavily on the traditions of courtly love that
flourished in France and England during the Middle
Ages. Perhaps courtly love had only a little to do with the

way any flesh-and-blood humans ever acted, but as a literary device it was one of history's great inventions. It
was a culture of restraint, but restraint of a kind that
implied rivers of urgent passion buried beneath polite
and elegant behaviour. Its rigid rules of conduct gave
intense meaning to the narratives that arose from it.

Scott didn't invent the idea of building vivid stories
around the mysteries and duties of knighthood. Long
before his time, tales of chivalry were lodged in English
literature, most famously in the legends of King Arthur
and Camelot. He drew his view of the past from literary
works that ranged from *The Canterbury Tales* to *Don
Quixote*.

But Scott was the writer who brought chivalry to life.
People riding on railway trains and living in terraced
houses were now speaking of chivalry — that was Scott's
work. The success of *Ivanhoe* encouraged him to write a
series of novels about chivalry, and soon they were being
read with excitement across Europe and on the other side
of the Atlantic. Over the years *Ivanhoe* has been the
basis of five feature films, the first in 1913, and two television series, but that's only the beginning of its effect on
the mass media.

Ivanhoe's ideals made their way into the mainstream
of modern mass culture by what might now seem an
unlikely route: through the cities and plantations of the
American South. From about 1825 to 1860, in the run-up
to the Civil War, Scott's books put down firm roots in the
South. He was hugely popular elsewhere, but no other
society loved him so much as the South. There was a

Northern bookseller who famously stated that for years he shipped Scott's chivalry novels into the South by the trainload. The Southerners looked into Scott's medieval romances and saw what they thought was a reflection of themselves: a courtly people, soft-spoken but strong, rich in honour, dashing and gallant. The Southerners already had pretensions to grand historic connections; now Scott gave them a way to connect these vague feelings and social ambitions to a grand, noble, and clearly Christian story. Southerners began to make pilgrimages to Abbotsford, the medieval-style house in which Scott lived, like Japanese in the twentieth century visiting the Prince Edward Island home of L. M. Montgomery and other sites associated with *Anne of Green Gables*. The Southerners borrowed Scott's flowery style in their writing, their rhetoric, and sometimes even their conversation. Southerners named their sons Walter Scott and their daughters Rowena. Strange as it seems from this distance in time, Scott's work became for the South in the middle of the nineteenth century what Victor Hugo became for the French — a symbol of what they considered their best selves.

Southerners, of course, were doing everything possible to create a distinct way of life that would justify the retention of what many of them knew was a great evil: slavery. They liked to call slavery "the peculiar institution," meaning it was theirs alone and could be understood by no one else. Scott's work was no impediment to this way of thinking. In the feudal times he depicted, men of nobility treated other men of nobility and their ladies with respect; they did not necessarily apply the same code to the peasantry beyond the castle walls. In the South, the parallel with white owners and black slaves felt comfortable; after all, in *Ivanhoe* the kings and nobles kept serfs, identified by metal bands around their necks. So Southerners could fit themselves into the narrative Scott offered.

In 1941, a North Carolina journalist, W. J. Cash, wrote in his wonderful book *The Mind of the South* that "Walter Scott was bodily taken over by the South and incorporated into the Southern people's vision of themselves." Scott gave the Southerners their social ideal, and they tried to live up to it by building pillared mansions with rose gardens and duelling grounds. Above all, they took from his fiction an ideal of female purity. Under Scott's influence, Southern men adopted the Southern woman as a mystic symbol of their nationality. As Cash says, in the pre-Civil War period, merely to mention Southern woman "was to send strong men into tears — or shouts. There was hardly a sermon that did not begin and end with tributes in her honour, hardly a brave speech that did not open and close with the clashing of shields and the flourishing of swords for her glory." Cash suggests that when the Civil War came, the ranks of the Confederacy went rolling into battle in the misty conviction that it was for her, the Southern woman, that they fought. He called their attitude "downright gyneolatry."

Mark Twain wrote, perhaps with a touch of hyperbole, that "Sir Walter had so large a hand in making Southern character, as it existed before the war, that he is in great measure responsible for the war." For Southerners who were readers of Scott, there was something noble even in a cause that was lost from the beginning; to Mark Twain, this aspect of Southern thought was "the Sir Walter disease." Idealistic chivalry coloured nearly everything that was said about the Confederacy's part in the war, whether or not it accurately described the way the soldiers actually fought. To this moment there appears to be an unwritten law that no one can write about Confederate soldiers without using the word "gallant." That's the result of Scott's influence: he provided the rhetoric that Southerners adopted as their way of depicting themselves — and to an astonishing degree, it took hold on the imagination of the world, a striking example of fictional narrative providing the frame in which we see actual events.

The Confederacy died, but Scott's spirit lived on. In 1888, Mark Twain wrote in *Life on the Mississippi* that while Scott's influence had weakened or disappeared elsewhere in America, it still flourished in the South, in all its "windy, wordy, flowery eloquence." Southern authors of the 1880s, he said, were still living in the shadow of Scott — and, as he put it, writing "for the past, not the present; they use obsolete forms and a dead language."

Even so, that might have been the end of the line for Scott, interment in the graveyards of Dixie pulp. So far as modern critics were concerned, extinction was his obvious fate. But the early twentieth century brought something earth-shaking, a new form of narrative: the cinema. It was the mechanical device that would take Sir

Walter Scott's influence to the end of the millennium and beyond.

One of the Southern romantics who fought for the honour of the South was Colonel Jacob Wark Griffith, also called Roarin' Jake, a cavalry officer who claimed to be a descendant of Welsh warrior kings. He had private as well as cultural reasons for doing battle: in the first year of the war his old Kentucky home, something of a mansion, was burned to the ground by guerrillas on the Union side. Roarin' Jake became the kind of officer who generated legends. It was said that after his hip was broken by a Northern cannonball and he could neither walk nor ride, he commandeered a horse and wagon and led his men into battle while seated.

With the Civil War over, he went home to Kentucky and fathered David Wark Griffith, who as D. W. Griffith was to become the first genius of the cinema. Within three decades, the heroes and heroines that Scott had loosed on the world acquired a more powerful and persuasive advocate than Scott himself could ever have imagined.

Griffith grew up in an atmosphere that sentimentally mixed medieval chivalry and Confederate gallantry, the purity of damsels in the time of Ivanhoe with the sanctity of Southern womanhood.

He seems to have been a born filmmaker, even though films did not exist when he was born. Certainly he learned early in his career most of the cinema's narrative uses. He wrote the grammar. He taught the camera to fade in and fade out, he figured out how to interrupt the long shot with a close-up, he worked with flashbacks and with shots taken by a camera in motion, and he learned how to keep two separate but related lines of action going at the same time, cutting back and forth between them. He demonstrated the way a director can guide the audience's point of view, selecting a facial expression here, a tiny corner of the action there. Under his leadership, films developed as an extension of novels rather than plays. The theatre places several characters before us at once, spread across the stage, and we choose what we want to watch. The cinema adopted the novelist's approach: it presented a single point of view and carefully selected what the audience was to see. By that simple stratagem alone, movies acquired a mesmeric force never known to the theatre.

These weren't all Griffith's inventions, as his admirers sometimes claim. Edwin S. Porter had used some of them in 1903 in *The Great Train Robbery*, five years before Griffith became a filmmaker. But it was Griffith who assembled them in the interests of storytelling.

What he gave the world was the reinvention of narrative within a new machine, narrative in the form of light etched on velvety darkness, appearing as a dream. For the audience it was an easier form to accept. We do not reach out for stories in the cinema as we reach out for stories in books. They come to us, their point of view already fixed by the director and the editor. This expanded enormously the audience for storytelling.

In Griffith's work, the defence of feminine purity became a major theme. In the early days he realized it through Gladys Smith from Toronto, who as Mary

Pickford became the first movie star of the world. Griffith further developed it with Lillian and Dorothy Gish, and in a few years much of the world had learned to regard ladies as vulnerable and needing protection, in the manner of Southern belles. This image acquired such power that it lives even yet, in private lives and public. Tennessee Williams put it to good effect in *A Streetcar Named Desire*, with Blanche Dubois as a pathetic, half-mad Southern belle whose universe of gentility has long since died around her.

D. W. Griffith also brought with him from Kentucky, and from Roarin' Jake Griffith's home, a more insidious and far more powerful set of impulses: anti-black racism. And when he set out to make his masterpiece, a movie that would run three hours with intermission and establish Griffith as the great artist of the new era, it seemed only natural to him that he should base it on a novel that embodied his father's view of life and his own background — Thomas L. Dixon's 1905 novel *The Clansman: An Historical Romance of the Ku Klux Klan*.

A South Carolinian, Dixon was precisely the kind of writer Mark Twain had in mind when he spoke of windy, flowery romance. Certainly Dixon would never have denied Scott's influence. The title emphasizes the main character's connections with Scotland — he's named Ben Cameron, a son of the clan Cameron. He also belongs to the Ku Klux Klan, whose members announce themselves by burning a cross, which is described in Dixon's book and Griffith's film as "the Fiery Cross of Old Scotland's Hills." Scholars have traced the cross-burning to one of the Scott novels, *The Legend of Montrose*.

So in 1915, when D. W. Griffith brought forth his masterpiece, *The Birth of a Nation*, it was heavily burdened by the arrogant and resentful racism that was the core of the Ku Klux Klan. A good many critics treated it harshly for that reason, and today it is never discussed seriously without an air of apology.

When Sir Walter Scott wrote his historical fiction, he was attracted to societies divided against themselves — Scottish nationalists versus pro-English assimilationists in his early novels, then Normans and Saxons in *Ivanhoe*. This was one reason the South had admired him in the first place. Later, movies about the Old West would follow Scott's pattern, returning again and again to the violent struggle between settlers and cattlemen — and of course, the most potent of all history-based films, *Gone with the Wind*, wrapped itself around the conflict between North and South.

The Birth of a Nation was a Walter Scott narrative separated from him by an ocean and a century, but it was recognizably Scott anyway. And it was also, in itself, the collision of two incompatible narratives. One was the story that Griffith had learned to accept as a child, about heroic white men defending themselves and the purity of their women against the menace of former black slaves. The other was the national narrative of the United States that was slowly being written, the story in which the South accepts the defeat of its prejudices, as well as the defeat of its armies, and all Americans go forward as one people, not as a nation divided against itself. *The Birth of a Nation* was condemned to be forever the site of bitter contention. Perhaps it was altogether appropriate that this great American work of art in the cinema should be entwined from the beginning with race, the great American tragedy.

Narrative survives these complex developments by evolving ingeniously. But there have always been challenges to narrative's central place in the human imagination, even to narrative's most valuable asset. For generations, its great accomplishment was verisimilitude, naturalistic illusion, and that remains in most minds its characteristic quality. When we praise a work of nonfiction, we often say that it "reads like a novel," and we mean that it reads like *David Copperfield* by Charles Dickens, not *Ulysses* by James Joyce or *Gravity's Rainbow* by Thomas Pynchon. We mean readers will be carried along by the flow of realistic storytelling and will be so caught up in it that they will, as we say, "lose themselves."

It is this very quality that from time to time has come under attack. Perhaps the German playwright Bertolt Brecht was the most articulate of its enemies. Why, he wanted to know, should we encourage audiences to lose themselves? Why put them into a trance? Didn't this simply prepare them to be manipulated and exploited? He wanted to make the devices of theatre part of what the audience sees; in his ideal theatre, the wizard and the levers he's operating would always be visible to, rather than hidden from, the residents of Oz.

Brecht set out consciously to destroy the power of fictional narrative in the theatre, and to that end developed what he called the alienation effect — which meant denying verisimilitude, emphasizing the fact that actors are giving a performance, and encouraging audiences to think about the material that is put before them rather than being captivated by it. But in practice, Brecht's theories dissolved. If audiences were asked to think, it appeared to be always the same sort of thought, something drawn from Brecht's bag of Marxist parables; and whenever a Brecht production worked on stage, it did so through the use of old-fashioned techniques that appealed to the emotions of the audiences. Still, long after Brecht's death in 1957, his theories cast a shadow over the theatre and other art forms.

One artist they affected was Jean-Luc Godard, the most influential filmmaker of the 1960s. Godard set himself up as the enemy of narrative in the traditional novel and the cinema. He remarked that every story should have a beginning, a middle, and an end, but not necessarily in that order; he specialized in fragmenting his stories and inserting little headlines that drew the audience's attention away from the characters and towards Godard's intentions. For a while, his work seemed a genuine revolution; but his influence subsided as his movies grew more obscure, and in the end all that remained were certain technical devices that other directors put to work in the service of relatively traditional narratives.

Fictional narrative encountered another enemy in the documentary tradition, and particularly in the person of John Grierson, a Calvinist intellectual from Scotland who invented the word "documentary" and later made documentaries commissioned by the British government. He was brought to Canada by Mackenzie King's government and made founding director of the National Film Board, which he ran from 1939 to the end of the Second World War. Grierson had a socialist's passion and a Puritan clergyman's grim determination to fight for what he believed was right. "Art is not a mirror," he said, "but a hammer. It is a weapon in our hands."

He thought of fiction as "a temptation for trivial people." He scorned Hollywood fantasies. Had he succeeded, he would have been a kind of antidote to his fellow countryman, Sir Walter Scott. Grierson did acquire followers all over the world, but the kind of documentaries he admired have never occupied a noticeable fraction of the screen time in movie houses or on television. His greatest influence was on the film industry of Canada, which was dominated by documentary ideals for years after he left and even now struggles to find a place of its own on the treacherous ground between fact and fiction. If the great failure of Canadian movies lies in their scripts (as I have often thought), that may be a historic legacy, the effect of several generations who devoted themselves to Grierson's desire for films that would work like hammers.

More serious dangers to narrative have appeared in the enlarging world of movies and TV late in the twentieth century. One is the tendency to bury both characters and plot in ever noisier and more violent special effects, in films like the *Die Hard* series and *Independence Day*; that seems likely to continue, and even expand, until audiences tire of it. Another is the strange spiral of paranoia-dominated stories that began in 1975, not long after the Watergate revelations, with *Three Days of the Condor*, in which Robert Redford played an intellectual in the CIA who finds that his superiors in the government are out to kill him. This tendency produced a few interesting films, and for a while seemed no more than a sideshow in public entertainment. But the American government has by now become the enemy in so many American films that audiences expect the villains of any given story to be representatives of Washington. The same tendency, transferred to television, produced "The X-Files," a program that might be classed as "paranoid paranormal." All the alien creatures that appear in this series have one thing in common: their co-conspirators are hidden in the agencies of the American government.

As the practitioners of narrative sought new ways to freshen their stories and keep up with the spirit of the times, they followed avant-garde artists of earlier generations and set about subverting narrative itself. Thus was born the "spoof," or satirical film, which is visually plausible but keeps signalling to the audience that we are not to take seriously anything that appears on the screen. No less an authority than the French director François Truffaut gravely declared that the spoof opened an era of decadence for the cinema. He wrote:

> The film that marks the beginning of the period of decadence . . . is the first James Bond — *Dr. No* [1962]. Until then the role of the cinema had been by and large to tell a story in the hope that the audience would believe it. . . .

Parody had been of only minority or snob appeal, but with the Bond films it became a popular genre. For the first time throughout the world mass audiences were exposed to what amounts to a degradation of the art of cinema, a type of cinema which relates neither to life nor to any romantic tradition but only to films and always by sending them up. . . .

No one was supposed to believe in the antics and mechanical devices of the Bond films, not even in the way we believed other spy thrillers. The producers didn't want us to suspend disbelief, they wanted us to laugh at their own work, seeing it as a kind of travesty. The Bond films subverted melodrama with comedy — not the elegant high comedy of Hitchcock's *North by Northwest* but a kind of smirking parody. That soon became a convention, moving from the Bond films to other spy stories, then to films of all kinds; finally, it became one of the persistent qualities in movies and TV. The essence of these stories was a joke shared by director and audience, defended under the name of irony. But what was the joke? What was the object of the satire? Perhaps it was the style of some earlier movie that took itself too seriously, perhaps it was the whole idea of melodrama. Sometimes the satire seemed to be directed at the very movie we were seeing.

The Bond films were often imitated but never lost their firm grip on the audience. Then, in the late 1990s, the form of decadence that angered Truffaut moved into a new phase, the parody of parody. Two films by Mike Myers, *Austin Powers* and *The Spy Who Shagged Me*, demonstrated that it was possible to satirize a style that had been a satire in the first place. Facetious or not, the early Bond pictures had, after three decades and more, congealed into an iconic mass of imagery — and from a distance in time, they now looked like monuments that a young comedian should set about disfiguring.

But a force far greater than any of these has for generations been altering the nature of narrative in mass culture and setting the style of the most powerful stories at the end of the century. When we glance back at *The Birth of a Nation* in 1915 we notice that it contains many seeds of the future, techniques and tricks on which movies would later be based and careers founded. We might fail to notice what it most spectacularly did *not* contain: movie stars. Some of the ticket buyers of 1915 who made *The Birth of a Nation* a success may have recognized the faces on the screen, but those actors were not stars. Griffith, the theme, and the grandeur of the movie itself — these were the selling points. At the time, Mary Pickford, Charlie Chaplin, and others were already established as independent names. As it turned out, the future of popular narrative films was to be their story, the story of stars, rather than the story of directors like Griffith. The stars were to be the carriers of the narrative tradition on movie and TV screens for the rest of the century. Critics could argue that directors create movies and everyone could agree that only good writers can shape good stories. But the camera and the projector steadily demoted both directors and writers by the way it heightened the emotional potency of the stars.

The movie star emerged as a new creature on the earth, a creature with a face the size of a wall and a set of expressions that engraved themselves on our memories more vividly than any books, paintings, or live actors seen on the stage. A new form of intimacy, or the pretense of intimacy, came into the world. We saw the eyes of the stars so closely that we could read whole stories in their glances. Their eyes, in fact, seemed no more than an inch or so from our own. Visually, we came closer to them than to anyone else except lovers, spouses, parents, and children. Movie stars (and, later, television stars) made this intimacy the foundation of their narrative power — and if they were still working over the same ground Sir Walter Scott covered in his romances, they were doing it in a new way, and with far more efficiency.

Quite early, it became clear that stars differed sharply from actors. Actors could shed their old parts once they had played them. Stars grew through the accumulation of parts, and as they began each new film they carried with them the residue of earlier roles. An actor's performance runs off after the film, like spring rain; the star's performance silts up, like gravel. It builds slowly into a narrative of its own. The admirers of Greta Garbo knew that she would carry her aloof beauty and her stern judgemental frown from one part to another, keeping them intact, as if they were precious objects she wanted to show us. When finally, in Ernst Lubitsch's *Ninotchka*, she played a stern Soviet commissar who learns to laugh and love in Paris, the central joke of the film depended on Garbo's history as much as on the character she was playing. The director, far from trying to make the audience forget Garbo's earlier roles, shrewdly emphasized her former persona in order to heighten the comedy. In earlier films, a star's image was sometimes conflated with the script's requirements, but *Ninotchka* made this relationship entirely clear for the first time. This was a film in which stardom became the underlying subject.

In the movies and in television, the lasting emotional power of a star blurs the line between narrative and performer, so that in memory John Wayne seems always to be working his way through the same western plot, from youth to old age, and James Stewart appears to be growing from a young idealist facing a grave challenge to an old idealist facing a grave challenge. In the process the character seems to learn little, but the star's grip on the part steadily grows firmer. Marilyn Monroe's wonderfully comic version of a sex goddess endures not because of the good directors who cast her or because of the scripts written for her, but because of the persona she developed. We cannot remember, without great difficulty, the details of any character she played; what we can remember is Marilyn Monroe, whose personality turned into a story all on its own, stardom overwhelming the films that framed it.

If we didn't know better we might imagine that each would-be movie star, setting out on a career, writes one master narrative to which all future scripts must conform. Jack Nicholson, for instance, would have outlined a story about a bright, funny, disdainful, sometimes angry fellow who cannot live comfortably within a carefully organized society and therefore ends as a loser while somehow remaining admirable, if only for his spirit. Nicholson brought forth this persona in *Easy Rider* and then kept playing variations on it until *Five Easy Pieces*, *One Flew Over the Cuckoo's Nest*, *Chinatown*, and several other films established him as a star — that is, an actor whose style is so dense and potent that it rises above the story and the other actors and lodges permanently in our memories. In the same way, Clint Eastwood has carried one powerful character from film to film over four decades, from western to detective story to political melodrama, from young, confident gunman in *A Fistful of Dollars*, in 1964, to old, worn, but still courageous gunman in *Unforgiven*, in 1993. At times his movies appear to be focused more on the development of Eastwood the performer than on the story he's enacting. Something similar happens on television, but perhaps with even more force, since the right actor in the right part appears again and again for years. For a large part of the 1990s, perhaps 10 million of us watched Andre Braugher as Detective Frank Pembleton in "Homicide: Life on the Streets," many of us remarking that he was the most compelling star in television. Pembleton became better known over a long period than any character created in a novel or play of the same period. And among all those who saw him, hardly anyone knows or cares who wrote the words for him to speak or the stories in which he performed.

The twentieth century has had many hugely popular novelists, from Ernest Hemingway to Danielle Steele, but it has no successor to Sir Walter Scott or Victor Hugo or

Charles Dickens. The novelist-as-titan has given way, slipped into the background. There remains much for the novel to do, and there are millions of us who want to read novels, but in narrative the centre of gravity long ago shifted to films and TV — and there the stars captured the high ground and seized the vast territory of the imagination that was once commanded by authors.

This has been the century of mass storytelling. We live under a Niagara of stories: print, television, movies, radio, and the Internet deliver to us far more stories than our ancestors could have imagined, and the number of stories available to us seems to grow larger every year. This phenomenon, the rise of industrialized narrative — storytelling that's engineered for mass reproduction and distribution — has emerged as the most striking cultural fact of the twentieth century and the most far-reaching development in the history of narrative. In this atmosphere, stars have turned into romantic heroes and heroines themselves, enacting their lives before us, following their own code, suffering and usually emerging triumphant. They are ordinary humans transformed by the camera into transcendent figures, carriers into the future of the precious flame of narrative, our epoch's equivalents of the characters Sir Walter Scott put into his books as the modern age of storytelling began.

This huge subject, narrative, never ceases to raise troubling questions, and the questions are likely to grow even more troubling as storytelling becomes an ever more pervasive aspect of life. One question, highly personal but perhaps also broadly relevant, concerns my own relationship with storytelling, and my fundamental need to consume and produce stories. Here the question can be framed in the simplest terms: is the impulse towards storytelling a sign of my mental health, or is it merely evidence of deep-rooted anxiety? Do I use stories to expand myself by making connections with others and to understand cultures that might otherwise be closed to me? Or do I use them mainly as consolation and distraction? And is there a way to distinguish between those two functions?

A broader question springs from the high density of storytelling in our daily lives. Mass culture and mass leisure have given all of us the opportunity to spend far more time absorbing stories than any of our ancestors could. Has this been to our benefit? Has it made us larger people than we might have been otherwise, or has it so filled us with aimless fantasies that we are emotionally and intellectually constrained? In this context, storytelling becomes an issue in the history of human development and democracy. Does our habit of seeing the world as stories make us understand ourselves better? Does it make us better citizens or worse? My experience suggests that it makes us better: narrative gives us a way to feel empathy for others. But it can work in the other direction, too. Narrative can make us smug by persuading us that we understand more than we actually do. It has ways of manipulating our consciousness. We have to consider the possibility that it misleads us as much as the white Southerners were misled by *Ivanhoe* and books like it in the first half of the last century; we must not cease to view narrative critically.

When I try to locate my own place in this vast subject, I see my whole life wrapped in stories — or rather, my *lives*, as son, brother, husband, father, reader, writer, editor, friend: in each of these, storytelling plays a large role. When I think of my relationship with my mother, what I remember first is her habit of telling me stories, which began when I was too young to read and didn't end until she was too old to talk. My first memory of *The Merchant of Venice* is her paraphrase of it, which she combined with an account of anti-Semitism. It comes back to me now, across six decades. The city of Venice, judges, Jews, a woman dressing as a man, and the quality of mercy — this cluster of images and ideas seems to be arriving in my childish imagination at the same moment, to be wondered over and then sorted out later, and then re-sorted again and again. My other strong memories of my mother include *me* telling *her* stories — about my friends, about what I had read, about the movies I had seen. She loved stories for the way they encapsulated worlds, and taught me to love the details as much as the themes. In early adolescence, I became a storyteller through imitation and through a conscious reversal of roles. Our love flowed back and forth through conversation framed as narrative. And if that was the case with my mother, it is less obviously but no less significantly the case in all my other meaningful relationships, including my relationship with the public during the half a century I have spent as a journalist.

Can we say that the triumph of narrative is a happy event of our time, or an occasion for worry? I doubt we can say either unequivocally. But we can say that narrative, after facing every conceivable challenge in this century, remains central to our existence, our companion, forever puzzling, forever irreplaceable.

BIBLIOGRAPHY

I: Gossip, Literature, and Fictions of the Self

Blatchford, Christie. "Rather Than Explain Her Life, She Rewrote It." *National Post*, 13 March 1999.

Griffin, Richard. "Johnson Admits 'I lied' about Vietnam Tour." *Toronto Star*, 24 Nov. 1998.

Kazin, Alfred. *A Lifetime Burning in Every Moment: From the Journals of Alfred Kazin.* New York: HarperCollins, 1996.

Linde, Charlotte. *Life Stories: The Creation of Coherence.* New York: Oxford UP, 1993.

Reynolds, Quentin. *The Man Who Wouldn't Talk.* New York: Random House, 1953.

Unwin, Peter. "The Fabulations of Grey Owl." *The Beaver*, April/May 1999.

Wilson, Edmund. "The Holmes-Laski Correspondence." *Eight Essays.* Garden City, NY: Doubleday Anchor, 1954.

II: Master Narratives and the Patterns of History

Coren, Michael. *The Invisible Man: The Life and Liberties of H. G. Wells*. Toronto: Random House, 1993.

Danto, Arthur C. *Narration and Knowledge*. New York: Columbia UP, 1985.

Frye, Northrop. "Spengler Revisited." *Spiritus Mundi: Essays on Literature, Myth, and Society*. Bloomington & London: Indiana UP, 1976.

McNeill, William H. *Arnold J. Toynbee: A Life*. New York: Oxford UP, 1989.

O'Donnell, James J. *Avatars of the Word: From Papyrus to Cyberspace*. Cambridge: Harvard UP, 1998.

Parkman, Francis. *France and England in North America*. 2 vols. New York: Library of America, 1983.

Porter, Roy. *Edward Gibbon: Making History*. London: Weidenfeld and Nicolson, 1988.

Young, G. M., ed. *Macaulay: Prose and Poetry*. Cambridge: Harvard UP, 1970.

III: The Literature of the Streets and the Shaping of News

Bates, Stephen. *If No News Send Rumors: Anecdotes of American Journalism*. New York: Henry Holt, 1989.

Brunvand, Jan Harold. *The Vanishing Hitchhiker: American Urban Legends and Their Meaning*. New York: W. W. Norton, 1981.

Burrill, William. *Hemingway: The Toronto Years*. Toronto: Doubleday, 1994.

Crick, Bernard. *George Orwell: A Life*. Boston: Little, Brown, 1980.

Elson, Robert T. *Time Inc.: The Intimate History of a Publishing Enterprise, 1923–1941.* New York: Atheneum, 1968.

Friedrich, Otto. "There Are 00 Trees in Russia." *The Grave of Alice B. Toklas and Other Reports from the Past.* New York: Henry Holt, 1989.

White, William, ed. *Dateline Toronto: The Complete Toronto Star Dispatches, 1920–1924,* by Ernest Hemingway. New York: Scribner's, 1985.

Wolfe, Tom, and E. W. Johnson. *The New Journalism.* New York: Harper & Row, 1973.

IV: The Cracked Mirror of Modernity

Boyd, Brian. *Vladimir Nabokov: The American Years.* Princeton, NJ: Princeton UP, 1991.

Cassell, Richard A., ed. *Critical Essays on Ford Madox Ford.* Boston: G. K. Hall, 1987.

Ellis, John M. *Literature Lost: Social Agendas and the Corruption of the Humanities.* New Haven: Yale UP, 1997.

McFate, Patricia, and Bruce Golden. "The Good Soldier: A Tragedy of Self Deception." *Modern Fiction Studies* (Spring 1963).

Seldes, Gilbert, ed. *The Portable Ring Lardner.* New York: Viking, 1946.

V: Nostalgia, Knighthood, and the Circle of Dreams

Cash, W. J. *The Mind of the South.* New York: Knopf, 1941.

Chandler, James. "The Historical Novel Goes to Hollywood: Scott, Griffith, and Film Epic Today." *The Birth of a Nation.* New Brunswick, NJ: Rutgers UP, 1994.

Dixon, Thomas. *The Clansman: An Historical Romance of the Ku Klux Klan*. New York: Doubleday, Page, 1905.

Millgate, Jane. *Walter Scott: The Making of the Novelist*. Toronto: University of Toronto Press, 1984.

Osterweis, Rollin G. *Romanticism and Nationalism in the Old South*. New Haven: Yale UP, 1949.

Schickel, Richard. *Intimate Strangers: The Culture of Celebrity*. New York: Fromm International, 1985.

Wagenknecht, Edward. *Sir Walter Scott*. New York: Continuum, 1990.

The CBC Massey Lectures Series

Also available from House of Anansi Press in this prestigious series: